THE DIVINE DELI

Faith Meets Faith

An Orbis Series in Interreligious Dialogue
Paul F. Knitter, General Editor

In the contemporary world, the many religions and spiritualities stand in need of greater communication and cooperation. More than ever before, they must speak to, learn from, and work with each other in order both to maintain their vital identities and to contribute to fashioning a better world.

FAITH MEETS FAITH seeks to promote interreligious dialogue by providing an open forum for exchanges among followers of different religious paths. While the Series wants to encourage creative and bold responses to questions arising from contemporary appreciations of religious plurality, it also recognizes the multiplicity of basic perspectives concerning the methods and content of interreligious dialogue.

Although rooted in a Christian theological perspective, the Series does not endorse any single school of thought or approach. By making available to both the scholarly community and the general public works that represent a variety of religious and methodological viewpoints, FAITH MEETS FAITH seeks to foster an encounter among followers of the religions of the world on matters of common concern.

FAITH MEETS FAITH SERIES

THE DIVINE DELI

Religious Identity in the North American Cultural Mosaic

John H. Berthrong

ORBIS BOOKS
Maryknoll, New York 10545

The Catholic Foreign Mission Society of America (Maryknoll) recruits and trains people for overseas missionary service. Through Orbis Books, Maryknoll aims to foster the international dialogue that is essential to mission. The books published, however, reflect the opinions of their authors and are not meant to represent the official position of the society. To obtain more information about Maryknoll and Orbis Books, please visit our website at www.maryknoll.org.

Library of Congress Cataloging-in-Publication Data

Berthrong, John H., 1946-
    The divine deli : religious identity in the North American cultural mosaic / John H. Berthrong.
        p.   cm — (Faith meets faith)
    ISBN 1-57075-268-0
    1. Religious pluralism—United States.   2. United States—Religion 1960- I. Title. II. Series.
BL2525.B49   1999
291.1'72'0973—dc21   99-039287
                                                CIP

To my parents,
Rhio and Donald Berthrong,
who taught me that the essence of
humanity and religion is a deep respect
for all other human beings

Contents

Preface

The Wonton World of Appetizers

This essay is a polemic concerning religious pluralism. It is intentionally provocative for the simple reason that I want people to ponder seriously the ebullient religious situation of the modern world. In a typically memorable turn of phrase describing the contemporary fragmented theological scene, the sociologist and theologian Peter Berger proposed that the modern theological turf is divided between the "uncertain-wallahs" and the "certain-wallahs." On another occasion Berger even more sharply separated the field into "thugs (certain)" and "wimps (uncertain)." According to Berger, the thugs are those theologians who loudly and vigorously defend all the historic dogmas of the tradition against any possible change. Somehow it seems to Berger that the thugs curse the pluralistic world too much, as if their sharp professions of undying faith were enough to ward off the relativistic evil of the modern world, rather like whistling past the graveyard. The thugs shout in order to drown out their own fear of change and the fact that they have no answer to pluralism save to reject it.

On the other hand, the prototypical theological "uncertain-wallahs" are so afraid of offending anyone anywhere that it is impossible to get a clear statement of faith from them; they are so timid that every living moment is governed by the fear that they might not be politically correct. Wimps will give no judgment about ultimate good or evil. If thugs yell too much, wimps are silent in the face of the need for the clear articulation of a renewed faith perspective. I understand Berger's own position to be that the truth resides somewhere be-

tween the two extremes of excessive exclusivity and fearful indiffer-
ence. Furthermore, a crucial field of battle between the thugs and
wimps resides squarely in the decision people make about whether
religious pluralism is good or evil.

Furthermore, the wimps are always on the defensive, always trying to convince the thugs that they are really good Christians. The
theological wimps have allowed the thugs to take over the definition
of Christian faith. What do I mean about thugs and modern theology? I will not prevaricate. I will give an example based on their
public statements and actions. As far as I can tell, a perfect example
of true "certain-wallah" theology is the doctrines and practices of the
leadership of the Southern Baptist denomination. Whether or not
the Southern Baptist leadership would accept Berger's description of
their motives is for them to say. Compared to liberal wimps, you
cannot accuse the Southern Baptist leadership of hiding their convictions under the proverbial theological basket. A liberal Christian
ought to have the courage to defend a more open view of reality, one
that celebrates religious pluralism and the crossing of old boundaries
as part of the amazing work of God's Holy Spirit.

But enough of castigating theological thugs for what they profess.
With some humor, my "certain-wallah" friends can at least claim
that they believe something! The intellectual turning of the other
cheek is the order of the day across the wide divide of fundamental-
ist, conservative, and liberal Christians. Besides, my attack on theological conservatives contravenes one of the wisest teachings of a truly
brilliant teacher, the late Professor Richard McKeon of the University of Chicago. McKeon, one of the team that helped to draft the
Universal Declaration of Human Rights, and no stranger to intense
theological and philosophical disputation, provided me with the following insight. According to McKeon, polemics are fun and that is
why we argue with each other so much. Notwithstanding the pleasure of refuting our intellectual enemies, McKeon maintained that
refutation of the other person's position is not the most interesting
aspect of theological debate. Fundamentally, philosophers or theologians are much more interesting when they are defending their own

thought than when they are attacking the positions of others. Besides, McKeon, always the meticulous scholar, said that we often fail to do justice to the position of our enemies. Better simply to say positively what you have to say for yourself. I take his point. I am not a Southern Baptist leader, to say the least. Therefore, I need to state my own position as clearly as possible.

One of the great problems for Christian theology today is the question of religious pluralism. Is it good or evil? What should Christians think and do about religious pluralism? College undergraduates know more about world religions and people of other faiths than the great theologians of the previous generation. My students are growing up with the Tao-Te Ching and the Lotus Sutra; moreover, they live in dorms with young women and men who are Hindus, Buddhists, Jews, Muslims, and even followers of the Way of Star Wars. Their rich experience of religious diversity and practice makes a lot of Christian theology seem quaint if not just plain silly. I sympathize with my students because when I was their age I spent my sophomore year studying at the University of Hong Kong. For the first time in my life I studied with Confucians, Taoists, Muslims, Hindus, and Sikhs. Just as in my own life, my students' religious experiences have gotten completely out of kilter when they confronted the accepted wisdom that God only works in the Christian church. Such an exclusive teaching simply does not make sense anymore, if it ever did in the first place.

While the various leaders of the established churches deal with the question by framing statements about their theologies of pluralism, something even more important is happening in the lives of people across North America. The churches are still trying to decide if other religions are worthy of their respect. However, people are crossing the old boundaries between and among religions in search of meaning and spiritual sustenance without waiting or caring much about what the churches say about their pilgrimages to other communities of faith. They are trying to figure out what experience and reason tell them about scripture and tradition. The most painful point of comparison is where tradition and experience meet.

It is common to decry the deli or supermarket model for such religious self-cultivation because it smacks of crass commercialism. How can we compare something as sublime as the religious quest with a visit to the local deli? For instance, I hardly ever hear a good word said for Shirley MacLaine and the New Age movement. The New Agers are believed to be simply too confused or befuddled by the richness of the modern religious world to be taken seriously. But this mixing of old identities is just what is going on even if it violates old norms and tastes. People are experimenting with truth, as Mohandas Gandhi wrote in a previous generation, because they are seeking the truth, and there are simply more options open to them in a free and pluralistic religious environment. People in North America are free to choose their own form of faith and even to mix forms that up to now had been completely separate and even historically antagonistic.

At some point the religious leadership of the Christian churches, and the other religions as well, will awaken to this new social reality. However, most churches are still at the level of trying to figure out what they make of Buddhism and Hinduism as a whole. The Christian world has not yet come to grips with the fact that more and more sincere Christians have practices, meditations, and marriages derived from the other historical religions of humankind. Hence, the official teachings of the various churches appear outdated, quaint, or simply incomprehensible to modern pluralistic Christians because such teachings deny the reality of religious pluralism.

For instance, to call your devout Muslim neighbor a pagan does not make much sense once you have gotten to know the reality of the faith of the family across the fence. To call your new Hindu dentist an idolater no longer rings true after she has told you about her faith in the God beyond all distinctions, what the great Christian mystics call the Godhead. Sociologists call this separation of reality and theory cognitive dissonance, the disjunction between belief and the facts on the ground. I suggest that the rupture and its healing have everything to do with the articulation of a strong pluralist Christian faith. Belief in the historical affirmations of the churches is not the same as a living faith, a faith that can make sense of the world around it without giving false witness against the neighbor of another religion or no religion at all.

Why should these Christians believe a theology that makes no sense to them in terms of their own experience of the divine reality? Why should Christians believe that God does not work in the history and lives of the pious faithful of other religions when they have seen the fruit of the Spirit in the lives of their Jewish, Muslim, Hindu, and Buddhist neighbors? If Christians discount the faith they have seen in people of other traditions, it is because they were taught that the essence of the Christian faith is to denigrate other religions.

When I attended seminary in the late 1960s we all tried to comprehend the teachings of theologians such as Karl Barth, a perfect example of a theologian who lived in total ignorance of people of other faiths. We marveled that someone as learned as Barth could write with such serene ignorance about other religions; even we had learned more as undergraduates. However, most of my seminary professors had too many Jewish friends to take Barth seriously when he wrote about other religions. Mark Twain wrote that when we say we believe dogmas we know contradict reality, we do so with our fingers crossed because in our heart of hearts we "know it ain't so."

Barth, in many ways an admirable thinker, and nowhere more so than in his forthright opposition to the Nazi abomination, rejected the vapid theological liberalism of his teachers during World War I. Unfortunately, this also meant that he rejected most of the reality of the modern world, including religious pluralism. Apparently Barth never even met people of other faiths. As Sallie McFague, during a recent Buddhist-Christian dialogue, put it, ultimately Barth had nothing to say about other religions or the ecological crisis because they had little meaning for him; he lived in a world untouched by sustained contact with people of other faiths. This is highly ironic because theologians like Barth claimed that they practiced Christian realism, reading the Bible and the daily paper side by side. I simply fail to recognize what is "realistic" about a theology that completely overlooks what is going on in the world in terms of ecology, the changing role of women, the clash of civilizations, or the irreducible religious pluralism of humanity because it does not fit into inherited patterns of dogma. It makes the Christian faith an object of ridicule for all the wrong reasons.

Is actually respecting the religion of your neighbor faithful to the received faith? Liberal theologians are asked this question all the time. My answer is easy: yes. For instance, we are admonished rather early in the Judeo-Christian salvation narrative not to bear false witness against our neighbors. Later we are told that God has never left the world without witnesses. Moreover, we Christians have been guilty of propagating all kinds of lies and distortions about other religions often based on a lack of real understanding or even deeper human contact.

But in other difficult cases Christians have now recognized that the tradition has been just plain wrong about all kinds of things. When the churches allowed the enslavement of whole ethnic communities because of the color of their skin and the subjugation of women because of their gender, that was wrong. I will not mince words. When I was growing up in Oklahoma in the late 1950s and early 1960s I heard from many "good" Christians that it was God's eternal will that African Americans not be allowed to own property in Norman, Oklahoma, or even have the right to stay in town after sundown. The only exception to this rule was made for the servants of the rich. Jesus was right that mammon rules when the saints are silent. As far as I know, all the rich people in Norman were good Christian folk. They and all of their preachers were dead wrong. Martin Luther King, Jr., proved that these people were wrong about civil rights and likewise argued vigorously for a fundamental love and respect for all people.

In the early 1970s I remember, as a seminarian and graduate student in Chicago, driving a group of resolute but fearful women graduate students to a restaurant in downtown Chicago that would not serve women in its famous lunchroom. I am happy to report that sexism died more quickly than did racism that day. The women, with some nasty looks but also some smiles, were served when they walked into that famous room with the long bar. Patriarchy was not so fierce that day. That these women were denied their full humanity until they protested was wrong. That women are denied a full role in the affairs of their churches is wrong.

How do we deal with this syllabus of errors? I have chosen only two, racism as slavery and the oppression of women, as blatant and quasi-universal examples of the gross mistreatment of human beings by other human beings. There are other forms of wickedness rampant in the world as well, such as the mistreatment by the rich and powerful of the powerless and marginalized. The list, of course, can unfortunately be expanded indefinitely. Human pride and willingness to denigrate other people are as universal as the commandment that we should love the neighbor and stranger as ourselves. The foremost thing is to remember that we are all under judgment. The simple Christian rule of thumb is to hate the error but to respect the person who makes it. There are enough planks in all of our eyes to give us plenty to do. Nonetheless, as generations of prophets have shown, evil must be confronted with words and actions of respect and wisdom.

In what follows I am resolutely open and positive about the fact that we live in a religiously plural world. Furthermore, thoughtful and sincere people increasingly are practicing different forms of faith drawn from the world around them. While there is nothing strange about there being many religions around for people to practice, it is still considered shocking in some circles that it is less and less strange to find a Zen Catholic or a Confucian Methodist than it would have been twenty years ago. Theravada Buddhist monks and nuns develop their own form of Christian liberation theology. Muslim women become feminists, and Christian women ponder ancient pagan goddess worship. African American theologians and womanist thinkers ruminate on the depth and significance of indigenous African patterns of thought and worship in African American religious communities.

Theologians, pastors, priests, gurus, monks, and nuns (Christian and otherwise) are being asked to advise laypeople who indulge in multiple religious participation. The old, historic, clear boundaries between and among religions are fading in the global divine deli. Not long ago there was, supposedly, a simple reply to such wandering between and among religions. It was wrong. More than wrong, religious wandering catered to the human weakness of syncretism, or in plainer words, the religious world often looked greener on the other side of the fence. Nowadays the common charge is not syncretism, a fairly technical charge in the history of religions anyway, but rather that we must not give in to the blandishments of New Age religion. We are told that to do so is to become religiously promiscuous. Promiscuity has never been highly regarded by the guardians of religious orthodoxy, and this would hold for Zen and Catholic priests as well as Protestant pastors and Orthodox rabbis.

Where to begin? Or, following the metaphor of a divine deli, what delights will we sample first? It has often been remarked, and it may be one of the few universal truths about the discipline, that all theology is autobiography. Or if autobiography, unless you are a saint like Augustine, seems just too presumptuous, confession is another way to move forward. Michel Foucault, the great modern French social critic and intellectual historian, remarked that the typical Western intellectual has been a "confessing animal" ever since the early Middle Ages. Autobiography is merely another form of the primal Western desire to confess our individual and collective sins to God. This fusion of autobiography and confession makes the launching point easy—I will begin with the person that I know best, myself. I do this not because I think that I am more pious or learned than other people I have met in the deli. Quite the contrary. I do so because I have been convinced by two arguments that have been directed at me from the opposite ideological ends of the religious spectrum.

First, our task is to honor reality as it is, true suchness as the Buddhists would say, the very cosmos of the creator God as Christians proclaim. It is the only creation we have, and if we are Christian, we hold that it is God's good world. We describe and interpret it as the human beings we are, or as a creature slightly lower than the angels and higher than the devils. If we take theism seriously, it is the reality that we incarnate and honor. To pretend that we have some other reality surrounding us is to be misinformed about the cosmos. It is a form of make-believe that gives religion a bad name. Over and over again my college students tell me that they have forsaken their parents' religion because it is phony. When I ask why they call it phony, they tell me that it makes no sense because it is completely fabricated, artificial, and does not touch on what they experience in their lives. Do they reject the search for the divine? No, but they would like it explained to them in a fashion that makes a minimal amount of sense. They would like it to connect to their own lives. And their lives include people of other religions, many religions, and no religions.

Second, at the other end of the spectrum, there are roving bands of philosophers who argue that all we have is ourselves and the living horizons of life, thought, action, passion, and reverence that spread out before us, in a buzzing, confused world. From Ernest Nagel, who tells us that we can never find news from nowhere and that all our news is from right here in front of our eyes, to Richard Rorty, who disallows us any access to sky hooks that will snatch us up and out of our world, to relativists like Joseph Margolis and Paul Feyerabend, who remind us that we are finite creatures who as much create the world in front of our eyes as look at it as something perfectly given for easy reading, these philosophers remind us, in their different ways, to pay attention to the real world. Pluralist and pragmatic visionaries such as William James and Alfred North Whitehead remind us that we are concrete beings living in a world of choices, processes, sunsets, and best of all, other people. It is, as James is purported to have said, when pressed to say if there was something more profound or unified at the base of the world, that no, it was just turtles all the way down. Just us turtles living in an increasingly complicated pond—at least to begin with.

Furthermore, third, there is a band of Christian theologians who argue that we begin from where we are because that is how God orders the world for us. We commence with ourselves because we are members of a community of faith that is rightly guided by the revelation and the sustaining presence of God. While we may not under-

stand the full richness of either God's revelation or the profundity of
our cumulative traditions, that is what we have to work with. To
pretend that we can step outside of our religious skins is not only
silly, it is misguided. We always start somewhere, and if you are a
Christian, you should have the courage of your convictions and admit that is where you initiate your journey. Hendrik Kraemer, the
great missionary theologian of the previous generation, and George
Lindbeck, a careful confessional theologian of this generation, cau-
tion us that religions are not something we can pick and choose at
will; religions are unified ways of life, and perhaps it is even better to
say that God chooses us through these grand and saving ways of life.
Kraemer and Lindbeck are nervous about all this chatter about religious wandering as if the world were really a divine deli. The choice
is more important than picking between pastrami and Montreal ko-
sher smoked meat.

Nor should such orthodox nervousness simply be benignly dismissed as the parochial misgivings of a few religious professionals.
Clergy have pragmatic and theological concerns that leap out of the
pages of weighty tomes and learned journals of theology. If the sheep
begin to stray too far, then it will be hard to fix the roof and to pay for
the wonderful residence and retirement fund of the local bishop. The
images are Christian, but they can be easily translated into the vocabulary and concerns of other religious communities. On the theological side, the really big gun aimed at religious borrowing is the
charge of idolatry. This is truly a serious charge if it is correct. Idolatry means to mistakenly or perversely worship something less than
divine as if it were the divine reality itself. In terms of modern philosophy, it is a whopping category mistake, the replacement of one
true reality with a counterfeit, bogus image of the divine or demonic.
As we shall see, I have a great deal of sympathy for the charge of
idolatry. We only have to remember the Nazis in order to realize how
horrific idolatry can really be. But the devil, as in so many other
domains of human life, lives in the details.

I have made it abundantly clear that I am a liberal modern Christian. Because of the nature of my life I have become acutely aware of

religious pluralism and how people are now choosing to practice different faiths. I have studied and lived in Hong Kong and Taiwan and I am fascinated and moved by Chinese culture. Most specifically I have tried hard to understand the three great historic strands of Chinese thought called Buddhism, Taoism, and Confucianism. As a national church executive for almost ten years with the United Church of Canada, I was asked to assist my brother and sister Christians in the work of interfaith dialogue. While I have had my doubts about what I have seen, heard, and experienced, I have been enthralled, stimulated, and occasionally filled with joy by what I have seen happening between and among people of different faiths and even no faith at all. My simple question is, What do we make of all of this?

I can only ask the question about the meaning of religious pluralism and the practice of borrowing from different communities of faith as a Christian. As Raimon Pannikar has argued, dialogue begins with a diatopical moment. Pannikar coined the word diatopical from two different Latin roots to indicate that we all begin in a place, *topos*, in dialogue with others, *dia*, in order to become fully human. Hence I can lecture to my university and seminary classes about what this means for other communities of faith, but that is only an educated guess, save for the Confucian world, which I have joined by study, respect, and reflection, not by birth or formal initiation into membership. However, I have discussed the matter of accurate and sensitive interpretation widely enough with Jews, Muslims, Hindus, Buddhists, Jains, Zoroastrians, Native American elders, Confucians, Taoists, and Shintoists to know that this question is not unique to the Christian world.

What culture critics call social location, and Pannikar incorporates in his theory of diatopical religious life, is important for my personal narrative. For instance, my African American and African colleagues point out that the sense of shock felt by Euro-American theologians when confronted with religious pluralism is passé from their point of view. The African American theological community has always recognized that they live in at least two worlds. There is the world they were torn from in West Africa, and there is the new

world, literally, of North America, the Caribbean basin, and the plan-
tation system of Brazil. In all of these settings, enslaved Africans
mixed their tribal religious cultures with the new religion of Christianity. African Americans could well ask their Euro-American brothers and sisters, So what else is new about religious pluralism in North
America? African theologians say ditto.

In order to be concrete, let me end with a story. In the summer of
1997, I had the pleasure of attending a conference on the rise and
flourishing of Buddhism in American life. It was a rich event given
over to fine scholarship and occasional musings from Buddhists about
how they see the Buddhist community developing in America. One
of the things that happened in a playful session was an attempt to
define what it means to be a Buddhist. Everyone got into the act and
we created new categories such as "bookstore" Buddhists, "nightstand"
Buddhists (those who not only have gone to the bookstore but are
now reading about Buddhism), and "friends of Buddhism" (people
like myself who love and admire Buddhism but evince no inclination
to convert to Buddhism).

This attempt to define the North American Buddhist identity
was done in serious jest. Nonetheless, even my Buddhist friends professed not to know quite what to make of the fact that it was harder
and harder to tell who was a traditional Buddhist and who was not.
The boundaries that seemed so solid between Buddhism and Christianity, for instance, were being eroded right in front of their eyes.
Although I will tell my story as a Christian, I am sure that others will
have similar stories to tell from their perspectives.

What has become clearer is that no one really knows what to make
of the new religious pluralism. The sense of unease is compounded
because it has become obvious not only that there is a flourishing
diversity of religions, but that members of these faith communities
are busy crossing old boundaries. In some cases, it now makes little
sense to talk about boundaries at all. One reason so many people
make fun of the New Agers is that the New Agers, whatever else one
thinks of them, cheerfully cross and often obliterate the traditional
boundaries of membership and confession that previously served to

define religions. Personally I get the impression that New Agers could not care less what others think of them, whether it be an orthodox Christian or a Wiccan bent on restoring the pristine European primordial nature religions to the North Atlantic world. New Agers are not interested in definitional religious purity; they are interested in the spiritual quest and what works for them. In this sense, the New Age movement only extends the American proclivity for pragmatism and willingness to defy European conventions.

But there is something else at work here. Much of modern theology resembles a traditional catechism. There were supposed to be set answers or at least sound guidelines for any situation. The problem with this approach is that, in honoring history, it pretends that everything has already happened that bears repeating. Theology is then reduced to a clever repetition of the wisdom of the past. But what happens when something new really happens? What happens when immigration laws are changed dramatically as they were in the 1960s in North America and Asian people brought their religions along with their electric rice cookers? What happens when people no longer believe that they have to drink at only one fountain of wisdom but rather are intrigued by the fact that the public plaza or suburban shopping mall now has a whole array of fascinating alternative water sources? What happens when people meet and discover that their Hindu neighbors are wonderful, spirit-filled people who have interesting things to say about the nature of God and even venerate Jesus as a divine savior?

What emerges from these questions is that more questions arise than a coherent collection of answers from the past provides. But then, in order to get the correct answer you have to know the right question. Religious pluralism and multiple religious participation define a new reality that challenges our old answers about religious identity and membership. Many old answers don't work anymore, or certainly creak with age. What we have to do is pose the questions to ourselves and pray for the discernment necessary to give satisfactory answers to them.

There is a profound difference between knowing the historical answers that a religion has given to the questions of the past and how it should respond to novel situations. In fact, real evangelism, as distinguished from revivalism, is precisely what is called for here. Revivalism relies on situations on which there is a culture and memory of the old religion that makes sense. But when the situation changes, and memories fade, there is nothing left to revive. Historical theologians are frustrated when pluralist thinkers fail to give clear and distinct, never mind socially hallowed, responses to contemporary problems. Conservative Christians understand this new positive view of religious pluralism as the mark of a lack of faith, a lack of knowledge, a lack of clarity, or just plain spiritual evasion or deception. The pluralist, on the other hand, wonders why the conservative is so sure that yelling out ancient confessions helps much. For the pluralist the question is the question. This is the smorgasbord of deli delights that lies before us now. The spiritual foods we choose will have a profound impact on religious life in North America in the new century.

In order to accomplish these ends, I will provide six different courses/chapters served from the divine deli and one offering of coffee at the remainder of the day. The first three chapters are introductory and methodological in nature. To make these bland formal theological and philosophical speculations more palatable, I will garnish these three chapters with numerous illustrative stories. It is in these three chapters that I will set the table and explain how the various serving dishes came to be there in the first place. The next three chapters will deal with specific case studies of interfaith marriage, meditation and contemplation, and the global ecological crisis. For instance, if humanity does not deal collectively and responsibly with the ecological crisis, there literally will be no more food for any of us. At the end, for coffee, I offer a short reflection on how we need to change our collective choice of food and table manners when contemplating religious pluralism and multiple religious participation.

To summarize, chapter 1 introduces the theological situation today via a short historical and theological description of the reality of the new religious pluralism. Chapter 2 asks whether pluralism will work on the level of religious theory and practice. It raises the question of theological judgment and interpretation in light of religious pluralism. Chapter 3 addresses the question of truth claims in a religiously plural world. This is the most abstruse material, but I continue to believe that we need to be truthful about what is in our minds as well as what we put in our food. Chapter 4 reviews the question of interfaith marriage as a matrix for transformational pluralism at the family level. Chapter 5 attends to meditation, contemplation, and prayer as venues of interreligious sharing around the globe. Chapter 6 focuses on the need for the religions of the world to work together to face the environmental crisis. The concluding chapter reviews the scene and reaffirms the thesis that multiple religious participation can be both acknowledged and appreciated by people of deep faith.

Other case studies about how people cross religious boundaries and transform inherited patterns of thought, action, prayer, and contemplation could have been chosen. For instance, the question of how religion should be taught in the schools of North America focuses attention on the changes that are emerging as public and private education confront religiously diverse classrooms. We can fear the new or delight in it. We can learn how to handle chopsticks and knives, spoons, and forks as we sample the divine deli. The divine reality has provided all of us with a truly cosmic gastronomic range of choices. *Bon appétit.*

Acknowledgments

I want to thank a host of friends and colleagues who have helped with the formation of this book. The first group was an adult education class on religious pluralism held at the Sorrento Centre in British Columbia during the hot summer of 1998. For a while we all thought that the forest fires raging on the mountains around us would swoop down on our class in religious pluralism. I also want to thank my Theologies of Dialogue classes at the Boston University School of Theology over the past few years for graciously allowing me to test my ideas and prose on them probably more than was warranted. More recently my Boston University research assistant, Mr. Gregory Farr, has been of great assistance in the final stages of the publication of the book. Of course, my truly major debts are to the Jews, Muslims, Buddhists, Hindus, Jains, Sikhs, Taoists, Confucians, and Native elders (and many Christians as well) who have shared their faith and visions of the world with me over the years on four continents.

One of the main sources of inspiration for the book derives from the work that I have done over the past four years with Professors Mary Evelyn Tucker and John Grim of Bucknell University on the theme of religion and ecology. Professors Tucker and Grim have worked tirelessly with Professor Lawrence Sullivan of the Center for the Study of World Religions at the Harvard Divinity School in mounting an exemplary series of conferences on the world religions and ecology; the series of books from the conferences will provide a benchmark for interreligious scholarship for decades to come. Over seven hundred scholars, representing the diversity of the religions of the world, have attended these conferences and have demonstrated to me the need to frame better theologies of understanding and cooperation between and among the faithful of the world.

Most pleasantly I want to thank yet again my good friend and colleague Dean Robert C. Neville, who continues to provide support, criticism, and a place to ruminate about the state of religion in the modern world. Professor Tu Wei-ming of Harvard University, one of my first Confucian teachers, often hosts seminars and conferences that remind me that the mind and heart can be vigorously and joyously conjoined in the life of a scholar.

Dr. William Burrows and his colleagues at Orbis Books have been valued friends on the path to publication. I am honored to contribute a volume to the Faith Meets Faith series. I am humbled to join such a distinguished group of scholars.

CHAPTER 1

Introducing the Divine Deli

California Pizza

On the Beach

Popular wisdom suggests that South Carolina is *not* a hotbed of interfaith dialogue or multiple religious practices. It is a state that defines itself with a robust commitment to evangelical Christianity. While Christendom has declined in most of the world, South Carolina is still safe for the monocultural practice of Christianity. Yet self-perception is notoriously deceptive; in reality, South Carolina is home to many religions of the world, including Native traditions, Judaism, Christianity, Islam, Hinduism, and Buddhism, to mention just the most prominent communities of faith. At the opening ceremony of the international meeting of the North American Interfaith Network (NAIN) in 1997, the Native women elders who led the ceremony remarked that it was a pleasure to welcome all the members of the other faiths to their ancestral home. Before South Carolina developed a Christian majority, it was home to diverse Native religions. In short, South Carolina has always been a multifaith region, even before becoming a state.

At the NAIN meeting, an outstanding and successful university chaplain told the following story. Like many pastors and professors working with college students, she had noticed that her students professed not to be religious while maintaining that they were passionately spiritual. That they would turn to her to talk about their religious lives proved their enduring religious commitment to the chaplain. The chaplain guessed, correctly as she got to know her students, that they were telling her that they were not very interested in merely repeating the religious practices of their parents. There is nothing surprising in this observation. Youth have, from time immemorial, wanted to break free of parental constraint. Alfred North Whitehead (1861–1947), a great Anglo-American philosopher of the previous generation, once remarked that the parents of the first amoebas to crawl out of the primordial oceans in search of adventure in the marshes and dry land surrounding the tide pools were probably lectured to by their parents that if God had intended decent amoebas to go on the land, God would have given them legs.

The chaplain told us that she had organized a successful retreat to a beautiful seaside beach in her state. One of the things that she did with the students was to teach them a basic form of centering meditation. It was a meditation designed to free their minds of the ceaseless chatter of everyday life, to allow them to enter into the stillness of the heart seeking divine inspiration or simply refreshment from the struggles of the day. She described to us the success of her program, and then remarked, "You know, this is really just *vipassana* meditation." She told us this because she figured that we would understand what she was talking about. We did. She was using a simple and effective form of centering meditation best known and taught in the modern world by the South Asian Theravada (meaning "Way of the Elders") Buddhist traditions. *Vipassana* meditation is widely used in North America by practitioners of Theravada Buddhism and is judged a highly effective way of introducing people to meditation and the calming of the excited mind. It both stills the mind and allows for the beginning of a Buddhist meditation practice if the person so desires. Moreover, it can also be taught to non-Buddhists interested in beginning their own spiritual journeys because it is so effective in calming the mind as the beginning of the path of spiritual purification.

What is fascinating is that this dedicated, young, and highly talented Christian chaplain selected a classic form of Buddhist meditation, not to convert her students to Buddhism, but to begin the reevangelization process of instruction in the Christian faith. She was trying to find a way to awaken their minds to the beauty of the Christian gospel. In order to do so she believed it worthwhile to deploy a meditation practice from an entirely different tradition, in this case, Theravada Buddhism. She told us that simply repeating old Christian stories to the students did no good because the students immediately identified them as the teachings of their parents. These Christian teachings were taken to be either boring or hypocritical or both. Whatever. Like St. Paul long ago preaching in Athens, also a university town, she used the best tools she could find from her culture to present the Christian faith. The difference is that the chaplain had an effective form of Buddhist meditation as part of her own religious background. Her religious world was even more complicated than St. Paul's, and Paul's world was complicated enough. It is worthwhile to remember that St. Paul used Greek philosophy while preaching to the Athenians about the new Christian gospel.

This story shows that the methods of Buddhist theory and practice have now become part of the Christian story and movement. Furthermore, because this story was told to an audience of the NAIN annual meeting that included modern American Buddhists, it crossed back into the Buddhist world, too. It becomes a Christian form of Buddhist *upaya* (or skillful means in teaching). The Buddha, rather like St. Paul in his willingness to be all things to all people, taught using a pedagogy that his followers called skillful means. The Buddha instructed, like any good teacher, based on his analysis of the intellectual, social, moral, historical, and spiritual condition of his students. The Buddha would have approved of St. Paul's suggestion that you can't give adult food to children; you have to teach skillfully and part of that skill is in knowing the background of your audience. Skeins of previously isolated traditions, in this case Theravada Buddhism and Lutheranism, merged into something new on the beach in South Carolina.

The Contemporary Theological Scene

Theology is concerned with God, truth, humanity—and all the other things that we bring before our worried minds and before the divine reality itself. If the monotheistic hypothesis beloved of Christians is correct, namely, that there is only one divine reality worthy of the name God, then God is the creator of the heavens and earth and all the things found therein. A person professing faith in one God can't be choosy about what she will consider; God is the Lord of all creation, and that creation includes all the religions of the human family. Three decades ago Bishop James Robinson challenged us to be honest to God about what we really believe as modern people based on the enduring truths of the Christian faith. The situation in much of Christian theology is even worse today than when the bishop made his famous challenge for Christians to think clearly.

The theological make-believe continues that if we just keep saying the good old-fashioned bromides all will be well with our individual souls and the church. Too many theologians ignore the facts of the world and pretend that theology is nothing more than recent North American or European intellectual history, as if repeating the past glories of the faith will protect them from their own time. Modern Christians live in a ghetto inhabited by the ghosts of teachings past; there is little creative engagement with the full complexity of the modern world as illustrated by modern science and technology and the persistent fact of religious pluralism. There appears to be little faith that God can speak to us in the present as well as the host of witnesses who have come before. However, before we can be honest to God we will have to be honest about the world, the literal creation of God and the only place we live. How can we even think of honesty in confronting divine reality if we cannot be truthful about the nature of the world around us? At a minimum we must be willing to open our eyes to see what is going on around us.

So much modern theology loses touch with reality because it does not tell the truth about the world. It refuses to look at the world as it is. Rather, theology tells us about a world that was once in our dreams or that we might want immediately, but not much about the world that we actually inhabit here and now. Nonetheless, theology is supposed to be about many things, including reflection on the divine reality that Christians confess as God and that such reflection ought to have something to do with the truth. Such reflection on divine things leads us to the conclusion that our notions of truth and God are not always what we think they are or want them to be. Such is certainly the case as Christians confront other communities of faith in the last years of the twentieth century. One thing generating a sense of religious crisis is when our understanding of truth about the nature of the world collides with our historical and theological notions of God. Of course, the very reason that this happens, if you happen to be a Christian, is because God is ceaselessly at work in our lives and our world. God is, for better or for worse, a principal cause of unrest, even for the weary.

The whole experience of the modern world has been a shocking one for Christians. With the collapse of the medieval synthesis of faith and life, many favorite ideas were debunked by the Enlightenment project of the eighteenth-century philosophers of France, Germany, and England. In North America, the Enlightenment project became part of the thought of revolutionaries such as Benjamin Franklin and Thomas Jefferson. The combination of critical and skeptical Enlightenment philosophy and the concomitant rise of science and technology spelled the end of medieval and early modern worldviews in the North Atlantic world. To doubt everything traditional was the order of the day. For instance, modern people no longer live in a triple-decker universe, with heaven above, earth (and a flat one at that) in the middle, and hell somewhere below. The simple world of God above and the rest of us below no longer makes sense; modern science tells us a remarkably different tale of cosmic complexity that befuddles even the most poetic among us. We float on a fragile blue ball in the midst of galaxies being born and dying in space so vast that it isn't even cold because of its magnitude. We muddle along the best we can. Closer to home, one of the irritating facts that has emerged for the Christian world is the persistent reality of other religions.

The older theory was that these other communities of faith were supposed to go away, yielding up their members to become new converts to the Christian way. A saintly and experienced woman missionary to India told me what she called a "tea story" about religious pluralism. Having as a young woman read the great theologians Barth and Kraemer on the theory of mission preaching, she presented Christ to the Hindu ladies of her new university and waited for their conversion. The Hindu ladies did not convert; they asked her if she would like another cup of tea to soothe her nerves. My friend told me that years later she told this story to the great Kraemer, who buried his head in his hands and said how sorry he was that she had derived this kind of mission theory from his books. Kraemer, who spent a lifetime working in the Islamic and Indic worlds of Southeast Asia, was shocked that listening and dialogue were not part of the missionary tool kit even if he prayed respectfully for the Christian mission of God to flower in the soul of every human being. My friend's Hindu friends did not convert, but they did come back for more tea and talk about God.

Another respected retired Canadian missionary to India told me the next "tea story." His intact sense of humor and humanity were evident in the way he narrated the story of his more than three decades of ministry and service in India. He said that when he first went to India he was convinced that he was taking the gospel to a new world. He fancied himself a spiritual Joshua; he marched the prescribed number of times around the walls of Hinduism, blew the right trumpet sounds, and waited for the walls of the Hindu city of faith to come tumbling down just like Jericho's did. He was surprised that not only did the walls not come down right away but the Hindus sallied forth with an invitation to tea. Somewhat in a state of shock, our young missionary went inside for his tea and, as he said with a twinkle in his eye, the real beginning of his Christian work in India began. He had taken the first step in getting to know some living Hindus rather than just chanting at them in English some theology learned in Canada.

The two missionaries from Canada drew the same conclusion about the real beginning of their work in India. Just tossing the gospel into the pond of Hinduism, as they put it, was not going to work. While Kraemer was no friend of multiple religious participation, or syncretism as he called it, he was a friend of dialogue based on reasoned theological convictions. Kraemer, after decades of work in Indonesia, believed that each religion was a profound way of life, complete and unique in and of itself. You could not take something out of Islam and put it into Christianity and expect it to grow—or so it seemed to Kraemer.

While I have always appreciated Kraemer's brilliant insight into the normative and unified nature of religion as a total way of life, I wonder how his theory jibes with the early Christian horticultural theory of mission. At least Jesus and the other early members of the Jesus movement loved to use the metaphor of grafting a wild olive branch onto the main trunk of a domesticated olive tree. The analogy suggests that multiple religious participation is just what we should expect in a religiously plural world. The proof is in the fruits and not in the pedigree of the plant stock. The problem is that if we think of religion as something fixed for all time, we will always be shocked by any new hybrid plant we encounter.

What the missionaries and Kraemer saw was quite different from what they had expected. One of the consequences of their work, along with the sincere presentation of the gospel and the planting of new churches, was the concomitant revival of other religions. For instance, Hindus, stimulated by what they saw Christian missionaries doing, themselves became missionaries, educators, doctors, and social workers. Some of these Hindu missionaries, especially after 1893, came to North America to tell their story in a fertile mission field. Even in the different missionary fields people have a way of participating in each other's religious lives. The Hindu missionaries borrowed the idea from the Christians that they could leave India and travel across a wide ocean in order to talk about Hindu *dharma* (the truth as an eternal way of life) with North Americans.

What is wonderfully ironic about the arrival of Hinduism in Chicago in 1893 is that it is precisely one hundred years after William

Carey, the great founder of the modern Protestant mission movement, sailed to India. What a difference a century makes. Now the most rapidly growing religions in North America are Buddhism and Islam. It is estimated that Islam, for instance, will replace Judaism as the second largest religion in North America in a decade or two. Though much smaller numerically, Buddhism continues to grow and fascinate many North Americans hungry for some new food from God's divine deli.

Returning to our contemporary world from the mission field of India in the middle of the century, the facts of the growth of other religions such as Hinduism, Islam, and Buddhism in North America are used to shock the faithful. For some people they, no doubt, conjure up images of Tibetan stupas or burial memorials across the village green from the local Southern Baptist church. For others, such demographic transformations bespeak a profound loss of traditional Christian culture. The great missionary movement of the nineteenth and twentieth centuries has turned out to have had some unanticipated consequences. Waves of the North American faithful departed to carry the gospel to the four corners of the globe, and they did so with astonishing success. Christians, who represented 6 percent of the world's population in 1793 when William Carey set out to India as a Protestant missionary, now account for at least 32 percent of the world's people.

Moreover, Christianity has now become a truly world religion with great and growing churches on every continent. Although the Christian churches are experiencing a relative decline in their old homelands in Europe and to a lesser extent in North America, I remind my students that more people are becoming Christians around the world today than at any other time in human history. But the communication technology and global transportation network that allowed for the miraculous growth of the Christian witness also flowed the other way. From 1893 forward, missionaries from the great religions of the world began to arrive in North America. The long-delayed change in previous racist and nativist American immigration policy in 1965 allowed again for significant immigration from West,

South, and East Asia. Christian missionaries and Hindu gurus, Buddhist priests, and Muslim imams now share the same Boeing 747s as they fly to diverse divine work.

Of course, Christians can console themselves that these numbers are merely relative to small, albeit rapidly growing, alternative religious communities. Given the small initial size of the Buddhist community in North America, it will be a long, long time before it overtakes the Christian church. But it is still there, growing, and perhaps even more frightening from a traditional, conservative Christian viewpoint, inviting many of the best and brightest young people into the ranks of its *sangha* (community). Along with being a rapidly growing religious community, the North American Buddhist community is the most educated group of believers on the continent. Recently a sociologist concluded that the Buddhist community goes off the normal demographic scales for personal achievement in terms of income and education in comparison to other religious people in North America.

Notwithstanding all this empirical data concerning religious pluralism, the main theological hypothesis to be tested is a robust form of monotheism. What does it mean to assert that there is only one God and that God is the creator of all that is? What does the doctrine of one God mean for the reality of religious pluralism? I will assume that God actually is God; there is nothing in the created order that does not depend upon God. Furthermore, I will deem that God, according to my Christian viewpoint, loves the world and is concerned for all its vast array of creatures large and small. For instance, in chapter 6, I will address the pressing contemporary ecological crisis as a way to expand our religious vision outward from the human community to the whole creation. Pressing on in a specific vein, God so loved the world that God gave Jesus as the Christ for the life of the world. My minimal list of key Christian teachings includes the incarnation, and the life, teachings, and passion of Jesus as the Christ. The key philosophic question for a theologian is, How does God relate to creatures and the creation?

One main task for theologians today is to explain religious pluralism. It is a key question if we accept that God is truly a creator god, and if we accept the plurality of different things, events, and religions set before our eyes in the modern world as the marks of divine action. Wilfred Cantwell Smith, the great Canadian historian of religion, once remarked that modern Christian theologians have better luck interpreting the origins of the solar system and universe than they do with explaining why the girl next door is a Muslim. Although I am not really sure that theology does a good job relating to modern science, I do know that theology hardly ever articulates a coherent, believable doctrine of religious pluralism. The religious impulse to accept the vastness of the physical cosmos has not been matched by an attendant willingness to greet peoples of other faiths as fellow creatures of God's love and concern. One of the things that most interested congregations I visited in Canada and the United States was my assertion that God was the God of Christians and other people. I discovered that many Christians actually believed this too, but somehow thought that it was a heretical doctrine or some kind of perverse betrayal of the Christian gospel. I always assured them that courtesy, respect, and love were never out of place in the Christian mission.

Another hypothesis to be tested is that the Christian gospel becomes more plausible for modern people when Christians look the fact of religious pluralism squarely in the eye and do not pretend that pluralism is only a provisional, momentary lapse, soon to be corrected by Christian outreach. Alfred North Whitehead once remarked that philosophers do their job best when they explain all the facts of a situation rather than when they explain away some facet of the world around them. Of course, such great feats of denial are common enough: no one likes those parts of a story that are too difficult, unhappy, or just plain out of place. We ignore the unpleasant and inconvenient. For instance, evangelical friends will chide me for only looking at the universal aspects of the Christian tradition and forgetting all the famous "hard" sayings about conversion and self-discipline. Notwithstanding this salient admonition, religious pluralism is not likely to vanish from our sight just because older Christian theologies have trouble explaining it. From a monotheistic viewpoint,

God created religious pluralism; our task is to try to understand it theologically, spiritually, and historically.

It is not easy for modern Christians (and probably not for any other religion either, but I do not pretend to write for anyone else) to make sense of religious pluralism in a positive way. Whitehead suggested a reason why this is the case. In contrasting the origins of Buddhism and Christianity, he wrote: "Buddhism is the most colossal example in history of applied metaphysics. Christianity took the opposite road. It has always been a religion seeking a metaphysic, in contrast to Buddhism which is a metaphysic generating a religion" (1996, 50). Whitehead amplified his meaning when he later said that "the Buddha gave his doctrine to enlighten the world: Christ gave his life. It is for the Christian to discern the doctrine" (1996, 56). Although Whitehead grandly calls this task metaphysics, what he described is something that followers of Jesus of Nazareth have been doing from the beginning of the Christian movement. The writers of the gospels, pastoral epistles, and Revelation and St. Paul himself constantly asked themselves, What does the incarnation, life, teaching, passion, and resurrection of Jesus have to do with God's love for the whole created world?

By this point the discerning reader will have grasped that I have tipped my hand. I not only accept the fact of religious pluralism, namely, that God really did create all of the different religions with their fabulous diversity, but that, like all of creation, diversity is fundamentally good. However, this primordial fact of goodness does not mean that there are no problems with the world. All one has to do is look around to make the informed guess that not all is in line with the desires of a loving God.

However, the doctrines of monotheism and fundamental goodness have certain implications for how I read the history of the Christian movement. For instance, it gives me a different reading of the "hard" statements about judgment and the exclusive nature of the gospel when compared to many other theologians. While this is not the place for detailed exegesis, I firmly believe that we must see the universal message of salvation and goodness as comprehensive and read the specific and exclusive texts in a pluralistic light rather than the other way around. I start with a God who created a good world; I then try to figure out what the specifics mean. But I repeat, this is not an essay in biblical interpretation. Anyone interested in a method of reading the Bible in light of our relation to people of other faiths can consult Wesley Ariarajah's fine study of various biblical texts published in 1985. My essay makes a prior move and takes the world as its text and focuses even more specifically on religious pluralism as a reality in need of positive theological, historical, and biblical articulation.

Another, less speculative way of looking at the issue was suggested to me by a Muslim friend, Professor Mahmoud Ayoub of Temple University. He noted that after 1793 the Christian churches had become a world religion in fact as well as theory. Prior to that time, Christianity was only the main religion of Western and Eastern Europe. Its scope did not compare at all with the international expanse of Islam or Buddhism. It was like a young adolescent set loose on the world in 1793, with all the joys and conceits of robust youth. But what happened next was astounding. This relatively small religious community of 1793 was soon armed with a might and power that would have astounded even the Roman Caesars. Somehow the church assumed that this technological, scientific, educational, medical, and military power gave it the right to ride roughshod over other cultural sensibilities.

Even though the mission of the church was carried out with the highest motives, it was not lost on the peoples of the Americas, Africa, and Asia that the gunboats of the European powers were always there to rescue the missionaries if things got tough. One feature of the story of the growth of the Christian churches from the sixteenth century to the present must be acknowledged. Who made up the bulk of the new Christians? The overwhelming majority were members of the indigenous or tribal peoples of the world. It has often been noticed how comparatively little success (numerically, that is) the Christian missions had among the great religions of Asia. The massive pool of indigenous peoples has now been missionized; one unanticipated effect of the rise of the imperial West was to provide unlimited access to the tribal peoples of the world. At the other end of the spectrum, the Islamic world has proved highly unreceptive to the mission activities of the church during the modern era. South and East Asia have also been largely impervious to the Christian mission.

It is difficult for strong and successful adolescents, such as the early modern Christians were, to recognize the feelings of other people. In short, my Muslim friend suggested that it was now time for the Christian world to move beyond its remarkable and powerful adolescence and recognize that there are other people in the world. It is time to grow up. Christians need a positive view of people of other faiths; and if that were not enough, we also must come to terms with the crossing of religious boundaries that defines modern religious life. Ignoring other religions and those in our own communities who have found spiritual guidance proffered by other teachers no longer makes any sense, if it ever did. Confucius once said that when you miss the target, don't kick it. Rather, look to your own conduct.

1962–1965: Into the Changing World of Religious Pluralism

Nothing in the normal intellectual patterns of the North Atlantic theological world prior to the mid-1960s demanded that theologians ponder religious pluralism. But three decades later a ride on the Boston subway should provide all the stimulation needed to wonder about God's prodigious love of different religions. All one has to do on the subway in Boston, Toronto, Washington, Chicago, or San Francisco is to look around at all the different kinds of people. When the ride is crowded, you even hear about Buddhist meditation or Hindu yoga sometimes; and all of this is done in the presence of someone reading her New Testament.

Like other people, theologians reflect the culture of their time. Most Christian thinkers of the 1950s and 1960s were dealing with an image of the world shaped by the vision of a triumphant Christendom. The missionary efforts of the past two hundred years had vastly expanded the domain of the Christian world, making what had once been the relatively small religion of Europe into the largest religious community the world had ever known. As I noted already, when the first Protestant missionaries (the Catholics, it is good to remember, had been in Asia for over two centuries before) sailed for India in the 1790s, Christians amounted to only about 6 percent of the world's population, and were mostly in Europe or a few of the European colonies in the Americas. Now, at the turn of the third millennium, Christians constitute about 32 percent of the world's people. As my Muslim friend said to me, Christianity, which had always considered itself a world religion, had finally become one.

The 1950s were a supremely self-confident time for Christians in North America. Theologians were convinced that the battle for the soul of the world had been won and that the dream of a Christian century was upon us. Actually, many intelligent missionaries, such as Wilfred Cantwell Smith, were, for a number of reasons, not so sure. Even though the twentieth century marked the greatest numerical growth the Christian world had ever seen, a missionary scholar like Smith was also confronting the revival of Islam and Hinduism in the vast subcontinent of India. Moreover, Smith, after having lived with Muslims in what is now Pakistan, was unsure that God was not also at work in the lives of pious Muslims. The old problem of religious pluralism would not go away.

Meanwhile, back at home theology went about its normal business of organizing the Christian faithful in the early and middle years of the twentieth century. One also should not underestimate the need for good home management. Religion brings out both the best and the worst in people; it can be demonic. In the case of "Christian" Europe, the most perverse demon was called the Third Reich with its racist and genocidal ideology. We are too kind to absolve the human spirit by calling Nazism a mere ideology and not a perverse religious movement. Far too few Christian theologians, with notable brave exceptions such as Karl Barth, Paul Tillich, Reinhold Niebuhr, and Dietrich Bonhoeffer, recognized the threat of the Nazis. For the Barths and Tillichs, Nazi thought needed to be confronted. In a later period, the Christians who struggled against apartheid in South Africa published a remarkable document that said, among other things, that it is the duty of the Christian to confront and combat evil, not dialogue with it.

One can only agree with those who fought the Nazis and later racist ideologies in North America and Africa that we must confront evil when we are convinced that this is what we have found. However, in the discernment of evil dwells a whole other story. On the other side of the world in the 1920s, 1930s, and into the 1940s, Mahatma Gandhi waged a remarkably peaceful battle with the English for the freedom of India. Gandhi once remarked, however, that he was pleased to be demonstrating against and fighting the English rather than the Nazis after it became clear that the Nazis were perfectly willing to practice genocide in the pursuit of their demented and vile aims.

Yet Karl Barth, probably the most famous Christian theologian from the 1920s to the 1960s, was of the resolute conviction that someone like Gandhi, simply because he was a Hindu, had no real place in God's final and true revelation. What was even more astounding, Barth claimed to know this a priori by the mere examination of his own theological understanding of what God revealed in Jesus as the Christ. One can only hope that God is both cleverer and more compassionate than Barth was willing to credit the divine reality to be for the sake of humanity. Better guidance was given by Pope John XXIII when he said that "in essential matters, unity; in doubtful matters, freedom; in all matters, charity" (Tracy 1981, 444, n. 33). Although the Holy Father was talking about debates within the Christian family of churches, his wise advice set a proper tone for any interfaith dialogue and religiously pluralistic society.

To be charitable to Barth, his real enemy, Hitler, was not the saintly Hindu ascetic Gandhi. Whenever charity wanes in reading Christian theology in the 1930s and 1940s because of its imperial and haughty attitude toward other people, all we have to do is remember who they were confronting, namely Adolf Hitler and all the deluded souls who followed his mad vision of a racist world. Yet, save for a few sporadic comments about other religions scattered around the vast edifice of his *Church Dogmatics*, Barth had little good to say about other religions. The very title tells it all: Barth was concerned with the reformation and sanctification of the Christian church, a church as much or more under God's judgment as any other human community. Actually, concern with the internal workings of a religion is a completely reasonable thing for any theologian (in any religion) to seek. However, the problem of coherence swells when internal reflection on the specific history of the community no longer jibes with the reality of the world. And because the world is always changing, theology must change as well unless it wants to become the mere history of religious thought and not the living articulation of the interaction of the divine with the created order.

Almost alone among his peers, Paul Tillich, probably because he fled the Nazis in the 1930s to teach in North America, noticed that the world was changing and thought that theologians ought to pay attention. At the end of his life, Tillich was asked what he would do if he could revise his great *Systematic Theology*. His answer was that he would rework the trilogy based on the encounter of Christianity with the other world religions. Tillich sensed that this was where the real theological action would be. It was no longer enough merely to tend the luxuriant garden of the cumulative Christian tradition. Of course, the same kind of ferment was going on in the Catholic Church as well, and it came to fruition in the Second Vatican Council of the early 1960s. The statements from the council were some of the first formal Christian statements in the modern world that showed respect for other religions.

The world was changing. When I point out that 1965 may be one of the most important years for religion in North America, my students look perplexed. This was the year when American immigration laws that had excluded Asians for decades were revised and relaxed to again allow significant immigration from Asia. Suddenly people from all parts of the world came to North America, bringing with them their inherited religious traditions. They came at a propitious time during the turmoil of the 1960s. Many young people were greatly disenchanted with all aspects of society, including their Christian churches. The grass definitely seemed greener over in the world of Hindu chanting and Zen meditation than at the local Catholic mass or hymn signing with the Methodists. Even the Beatles learned how to play the sitar. Furthermore, the civil rights movement led by great African American religious leaders such as Martin Luther King, Jr., and Malcolm X, one Christian and one Muslim, witnessed to the dream for a new world of racial and religious diversity and harmony.

Along with the transformation of the American immigration scene, another sea change occurred on 28 October 1965 a world away in Rome. In the great Second Vatican Council (1962–65) of the Roman Catholic Church, the largest single Christian church declared a positive regard for the religions of humankind in its famous conciliar decree *Nostra Aetate*. For a tradition, and here the Roman Catholics shared a common sentiment with their Protestant and Orthodox sisters and brothers, that had taught that outside the church there was no salvation since the First Vatican Council in 1442, this was a major transformation. The Roman Catholic Church has a wonderfully supple and creative way of seeing the organic growth of tradition. The intent of the fathers of Vatican II was clear: it was and remains an impressive teaching of respect for other religious communities.

Incontestably, among the Christian family of churches, the Roman Catholics have led the movement toward better understanding and appreciation of other religions. Roman Catholics can proudly point to the work of creative early missionary scholars such as Robert de Nobili in India and Matteo Ricci in China as sources for an enlightened view of the religions of the world. De Nobili and Ricci proved that you can have the highest respect for another tradition and still retain unshakable commitment to your own faith. But what is even more fascinating, as Lionel Jensen (1997) has argued so passionately, is that we find a genuine mutual transformation in Ricci's thought and life brought about by his contact with Chinese culture. Ricci developed a profound respect for Confucianism as a philosophy; Confucians repaid him by calling him a Western Confucian. Multiple religious or worldview participation does not mean that all elements of the new synthesis have an equal weight, however. Ricci loved the Confucian classics but remained one of the greatest Roman Catholic missionaries of all times.

It is difficult to overestimate the impact of *Nostra Aetate* for the Christian world. The formal statement is short. We are told that it began life as part of the larger draft statement on Christian ecumenism. But it became clear that although ecumenism, that is to say, internal Christian relations, and interreligious concerns are intimately inter-related, they are separate in fundamental aspects. There is a great deal of difference between "separate brethren," non–Roman Catholic fellow Christians, and Hindu ascetics, Confucian scholars, Muslim theologians, Jewish rabbis, Shinto priests, and Buddhist monks. However, under the pontificate of John XXIII, there was one common characteristic of the Vatican II documents, namely, charity toward all people. One wishes that such a feeling of goodwill and charity would pervade all the interactions of religious communities.

The World Council of Churches, representing many Protestant, Anglican, and Orthodox communions, has been slower to embrace the new spirit of interreligious reconciliation in its formal pronouncements. One pragmatic reason for this reticence is the composite, conciliar nature of the WCC. The WCC is not a single superchurch; it is a council and cannot do more than speak for the consensus of its member communions and denominations. Across the board these denominations are still having trouble deciding if other religions are works of God or something more misguided or even demonic. It is ironic that the churches of the Protestant Reformation are now the very Christian bodies that are unsure that God is creative or loving enough to work outside of their all-too-human social boundaries. They seem to affirm a kind of credit card view of reality: God will only take a Visa card to get you into the Kingdom of Heaven, and it doesn't hurt if it is a gold or platinum card as well. Members of MasterCard, American Express, or Discover, it appears, need not apply for membership in the divine fellowship.

The world has changed even if the various Christian churches and theologians have been unable to adjust to the change. Of course, there are Christians who argue that any significant change in the basic doctrine would be a betrayal of the historical faith of the church, the very deposition of belief that has rightly guided Christians down through the centuries. Whitehead observed that "a system of dogmas may be the ark within which the Church floats safely down the flood-tide of history. But the Church will perish unless it opens its windows and lets out the dove to search for an olive branch" (1996, 145–46). The other point that Whitehead does not mention is that the ark will probably begin to stink if the windows are not opened and some new air is allowed to blow through.

Another way to look at the problem is to use the notion of the Big Bang theory of creation as proposed by modern physicists. Many religious people believe that religion is like the Big Bang itself. The closer you are to the beginning, the closer you are to God's decisive acts. This is the reason that Christians of all ideological stripes are so interested in the Bible. Using the analogy of the inception of the universe, the New Testament is as close as we can get to Jesus, so we need to study it in order to engage the beginning of our religion. However, this is an odd way to look at the monotheistic faith taught by Jesus. If God is God, is not God as close to us as to anyone living in the Galilee of Jesus in the first century? It is salutary to remember that some of the earliest writings we have, the letters of St. Paul, were written by someone who never actually met the living Jesus. St. Paul's encounters were all with the living Christ of faith. If we were strict Big Bang theorists, we should try to get behind St. Paul to the reality of the actual incarnation. However, this theological vision ignores the fact that God's Holy Spirit blows where and when it will.

Nonetheless, the counterclaim is that dogmas were received complete as inspired teachings delivered once and for all by the early church (pick your favorite end point here, depending on your denomination) and are the necessary skeleton upon which the living flesh of the faithful is arranged. All of this is true, but candor demands that we admit that dogmatic teachings change over time as well. For instance, no one seriously defends slavery as a moral system anymore, though it was commonly accepted in the ancient world.

Moreover, few people now defend the senseless subjugation of women in the name of Christian dogma, though this raises more debate than the question of slavery. Nonetheless, the point is clear. Ideas change over time. Slavery was once acceptable. It no longer is. The denigration of women has been a theme of history since the Neolithic. But now many women and men are challenging the inherited wisdom about the role of women in the modern world. Feminists argue that patriarchy will soon join slavery on the dust heap of history.

Some people will not be persuaded by historical arguments. They will counter that the modern world has brought us the horrors of the Shoah, the death camps of Cambodia, the sectarian violence of the Middle East, the racism of the American south, and the genocide of Rwanda. This is, of course, only a partial list of the blind fury of the demonic in the twentieth century. They point to the fact that teachings about truth, love, and justice may be all that raises the beacon of decency in a depraved world, and that we had better leave well enough alone. Furthermore, they will rightly argue that the Nazis worked closely with Christians and that some Christians were seduced into changing the ethical teachings of the church to suit the goals of Hitler and his cronies.

This is true. Religious history entombs the best and worst of human nature. One claim is that dogmas, in all religions, bespeak what is good, what is divine, and what is true. These norms of faith, meditation, prayer, ritual, and ethical practice enshrine the only connection that we have with the divine reality. We tamper with divine guidance to our own detriment. Yet the dogmas change and some are simply abandoned, like the defense of slavery within civilized society. A Jesuit colleague once remarked to me that when and if the Roman Catholic Church decides to ordain women, the encyclical will begin with the tested formula, "As the Holy Catholic Church has always and everywhere taught . . ." The polite way to save face is to say that dogmas don't really change, they just develop different or unexpected manifestations to meet the needs of new historical realities.

The common denominator that lurks behind all of these arguments about the plasticity of dogma is ethical reflection on the role dogma plays in the actual lives and actions of people and nations. There is a nagging, almost visceral, feeling that something has gone wrong when the tradition teaches a theory that flies in the face of ethical conduct, much less practical reality. The empirical fact that the girl next door in modern North America might well be a Hindu or Buddhist makes the old view of Hinduism and Buddhism as reprehensible teachings less and less appealing. All the more so when your son falls in love with Ms. Tara and you now have a perfectly wonderful Buddhist daughter-in-law. If your brilliant and gentle new dentist is a Muslim, older Christian notions about the depravity of her faith may seem a touchy subject as you begin a root canal. Empirical pragmatics join common sense and ethical prudence to cause you to rethink the historic negative Christian teachings about the nature of the Qur'an and the role of Muhammad as a prophet of God.

There is yet another empirical and historic reality that Christians must confront in the pluralistic world of the global nightly news channel that never sleeps. It has been hard for many Christians to abandon an imperial view of their faith, to abjure the hegemonic idea of Christendom. Christendom was the image of a world controlled completely by Christian countries. Arthur Koestler, no fan of multiculturalism, remarked that many Western Christians approached other peoples "armed with gun-and-gospel truth" (Clarke 1997, 7). The outcome of joining modern military and economic superiority with religious atavism was a form of Christofascism. This is a hard term, one that jolts our sensibilities if we are Christian. How can we link Christ with the hateful attitudes of fascist doctrine? People who have suffered indignities at the hands of Christians during the past four centuries want us to remember how our imposition of culture and faith appeared to them. Many other people want Christians to recognize and then renounce this part of Christian history before meaningful dialogue can begin.

One of the main ways to uncouple doctrine and practice is to reject intolerance. If we aren't sure what dogmas we need to preserve, we can at least try to act with compassion and insight. We need a more flexible way to approach differences between and among religions, especially in a day when people are moving so rapidly between what formerly were rigid religious identities. As Whitehead wrote in the 1930s, "Intolerance is the besetting sin of moral fervour" (1933, 63). Jesus himself was somewhat more tolerant than his followers have been. Yet Whitehead also noted that "at the period of the Reformation mankind has begun to know better and so charity of judgment upon the Reformers begins to wear thin. But then charity is a virtue allied to tolerance, so we must be careful" (ibid.).

I believe that the problems and joys of religious pluralism come to us because of the reality of people living with us in our own communities and because much of our inherited theology does not help us deal with these people. Religions waver between being great universal messages of salvation and the specific practices and ideas of particular groups of gathered worshipers. We must look within the universal and specific features of our religions in order to deal effectively with the challenge of pluralism. The challenge is ultimately ethical and theological. In fact, it is always almost impossible to sever the link of ethics and theology. Does religion, my students ask, always have to be linked to hatred and exclusivistic theological claims that cut like a knife?

I recall sitting with a refugee Tibetan family during a visit of the Dalai Lama, the revered leader of the Tibetan people who has been in exile since the Chinese occupation of Tibet in 1959, in a great Anglican cathedral in Toronto in the early 1980s. I remember especially the joy of the little Tibetan girl in seeing her great teacher welcomed by many Christian leaders. However, the service was disrupted by a Christian zealot who shouted out curses at the Dalai Lama and the Christians who had allowed a non-Christian, a pagan, and an idolater to profane such holy space. My little neighbor kept asking why this person hated the Dalai Lama and had she done anything wrong by coming to the church. A wonderful couple were sitting by me and the family. I confess I thought of them as a perfect example of the Canadian Anglican elite. They were impeccably and elegantly dressed and spoke to each other in hushed, educated tones with a slight English accent. They immediately rushed to the comfort of the little girl and her family. When it was all over, the lady turned to her husband and said ever so quietly, "Well, I guess that kindness is no longer a Christian virtue. I had always thought we were supposed to welcome the stranger from a far land." I was proud of that lady and her husband.

I doubt that the couple knew very much about the Tibetan Buddhist tradition. By now, however, it is hard not to know something about the Dalai Lama. The Anglican couple came, as far as I could tell, to show a gracious welcome to another person of faith, a person who was struggling to lead his community in the wilderness of their exile. They were not there to judge the soul of the Dalai Lama, but they were prepared to offer immediate assurance to a little girl who felt threatened by the rude actions of another Christian. I don't like to play the game of "what would Jesus have done in this situation?" However, I am mortally convinced that Jesus would have comforted the little girl—as far as I know, not even the most skeptical scholar of the New Testament has ever doubted that Jesus had a special place in his heart for children. Whatever else Christian theology must be, it must be moral. It should never be used to frighten a little girl far from her native land.

CHAPTER 2

Will a Deli Really Work?

Choosing the Pastrami

The 16 January, 1998, issue of the *Chronicle of Higher Education* ended with an editorial about religious revivals and activities on college campuses. The *Chronicle* is the publication of record for the academic community. It contains all the gossip about what is going on in the various disciplines, colleges, and universities, both in the United States and around the world, as well as job listings for positions all over the world. It even has a sports page, believe it or not. The editorial for that day began: "While conducting research for a project on work and spirituality, I asked a recent college graduate what her religious preference was. 'Methodist, Taoist, Native American, Quaker, Russian Orthodox, and Jew,' she answered with an easy laugh." Professor Diane Winston drew the correct conclusion that "we no longer live in a Christian nation, or even a Judeo-Christian one."

When people talk to college students about their religious commitments they find that many students vehemently deny that they are religious but will declare that they are spiritual. Nor is this denial of "religion" confined to college students. I have heard similar comments all over North America from the young, the middle-aged, and the elderly. Because this denial of religion yet affirmation of spirituality appears to be a contradiction of sorts, further dialogue is required. When researchers probe deeper, they discover that students' "spirituality" and being spiritual means rejecting any easy identification with the religious practice of their parents. In most respects there is nothing astounding in this profound disgruntlement with the religious status quo; young people have from time immemorial sought to distance themselves from their families as part of finding their own place in the world. What is more interesting is that they resolutely affirm a spiritual dimension to their life. Much the same thing has been told to me by older people, though they are no longer rebelling against their parents; they have simply become bored with or disillusioned by their traditional churches. They are seekers, and there is a lot to be found these days beyond that "old-time religion." The New Age is with us in all its gaudy profusion of symbols and fads.

Along with the New Age we have all other kinds of religions, too. With the changing demography of North America almost every major or minor city has synagogues (and probably has had for a long time), new Islamic centers, Hindu shrines, and Buddhist temples. Moreover, the Jewish, Muslim, Hindu, and Buddhist centers are growing communities of faith that have extensive outreach to people beyond their own congregations. With the intense interest North Americans have in all kinds of religion, it would be almost impossible not to develop some form of external mission. Some Taoists recently told me that although their specific denomination was dedicated to a retiring life in China, they too had to formulate a way to cope with the sincere interest in their ancient tradition on the part of many North Americans. This kind of unanticipated religious notoriety is a common theme when you talk to the representatives of the new religious mosaic of North America (many of whom point out that they have actually been here for a long time, even if in relative obscurity compared to the larger Christian churches).

Of course, one way to dismiss this new wave of spiritual seeking is to reject it as mindless syncretism or as nothing but New Age froth. This is the strategy that if we ignore something we do not like, it will go away. Of course, one person's froth is another person's full-course meal. Within the world of New Age religion and the revival of older, pre-Christian forms of European worship there are whole levels of knowledge and commitment. Because of the accidents of personal friendship, over the years I have had the opportunity to talk to many followers of what they call the Craft or Wicca. In common parlance this is witchcraft. Odd as it may seem, members of this particular new religious movement adamantly deny that they are New Age. They believe that they are reviving, in various ways, the traditional religious lore and profound religions of nature of the European past before the rise of Christianity.

Driven by an awareness of the ecological crisis, Wiccans strive to revive the primal nature religions of the European peoples. My Wiccan friends find the divine in the appreciation and worship of nature; they argue that Christianity is so invested in trying to escape the world that it has lost any connection to the magic of this world. Moreover, they understand that they have a broken tradition and that they have to reconstruct their way of life out of assorted dim memories. The best Wiccan theologians realize that they retain only bits and pieces of what were once whole religions; from the Wiccan point of view, all of their sacred history was erased by the arrival and hostility of the Christian missionaries and feudal warriors who were the military arm of the church. Nonetheless, for them these ancestral memories of the earth and its sacred stories ought not to be ignored, but in fact, need to be revived for the good of all humanity and the earth itself.

We encountered the term *syncretism* before. It means many things to many people, but it is fair to say that for most modern Christians, if they think about it at all, syncretism has taken on a pejorative meaning. Some scholars of religion have tried to rescue syncretism from the disdain of theologians, but with little success. That words transform meanings over time is hardly unusual. J. J. Clarke, the English historian of the impact of Asian thought on the West, has pointed out that for many eighteenth-century Enlightenment thinkers the word *despot* meant a good and worthy ruler under certain conditions. Some Enlightenment philosophers were in favor of despots in the same way modern English speakers are generally in favor of democratic institutions as icons of just government. However, unlike the Red Queen in Alice's famous adventures, we cannot always wish a word to mean what we say it does.

What syncretism means in the history of religion is actually quite simple. It is a theory that maintains that some religious leaders consciously borrow ideas, practices, prayers, vestments, rituals, and so on, from two or more different religions and concoct a completely new religion out of the various older parts. Interestingly enough, there are very few examples of stable syncretism in the religious history of humankind. An important exception was the new religion founded by the prophet Mani. Mani was born in Babylonia in 216. In 228, Mani began to receive revelations. In content and structure, Mani's revelations were closely related to a number of religious movements current in the world of the Middle East during the third century of the Common Era. For instance, Mani made use of certain heretical Christian sectarian ideas about things like spirit and matter to help create his new religion. The essence of his teaching was a cosmic religious dualism, a dramatic battle between the forces of good and evil. The Manichaean church was made up of the Elect and the Auditors. The Elect were the truly sanctified; they were the leaders and were considered the pure ones destined to escape the toils of this evil, corrupt world. Mani's new religion was a highly successful invention.

Why dwell on such an ancient example? Even though Mani's religion, after a very successful start, eventually died out and was replaced by orthodox Christianity and later by Islam in the Middle East, its influence continues to live on in the Christian West. The reason is because St. Augustine, during the early part of his search for the City of God, dabbled in Manichaeanism. Later in his life Augustine denied any lasting impact of Mani's faith on his own religious thought, but scholars are not so sure. The heavy dualism of spirit and matter, reason and passions, good and evil betrays something of the Manichaean vision lurking in Augustine's final vision of the Christian faith. Hence, we can say that syncretism had an impact on the formation of early Western theology through the life and thought of Augustine.

From a Jewish perspective, Christianity was a strange syncretistic religion in and of itself. As the early Jesus movement became the gentile Christian church, it separated itself further and further from its Jewish roots in doctrine and practice. The very act of recording its distinctive sacred books in Greek rather than Hebrew was a syncretic one. Andrew Walls, the doyen of Christian mission historians, makes the point that the very first anonymous Christian missionaries we encounter in the Acts of the Apostles began the whole history of Christian mission and the foundation of the gentile church by translating the Jewish notion of the Messiah into the Greek term *Christ* for the sake of their gentile friends in Antioch. The term *Christ* or *Lord* was common in the Greek-speaking world of the first century and was employed by many current religious movements to designate their understanding of the highest form of divinity. It was a choice that worked, and we find that St. Paul, the best known of the early missionaries of the Jesus movement, continued to use the term *Christ* to explain the life, teachings, death, and resurrection of Jesus to his gentile and Greek-speaking audience.

Having had a great deal of luck with the use of Greek terminology in generating a Greek-speaking church, the early Christian theologians proceeded to explain what had begun as a Jewish movement in rural Galilee in terms of the most up-to-date Greek metaphysical categories. The Greek fathers skillfully borrowed their philosophies and terminology from older Platonic, Neoplatonic, Stoic, and Aristotelian sources. They were so successful that the Jewish roots of the Christian faith were often denied completely. St. Jerome completed the transformation by creating a beautiful Latin translation of the Christian scriptures that became the canonical word of God and source for the divine liturgy for the Western Roman Catholic Church down to the middle of the twentieth century.

The point is that all religions are syncretistic to some degree. However, very few religions like to admit as much even if they do carry off any good idea that is not bolted down. And if we think that such borrowing only went on at the beginning of a new religion, we need to think again. For instance, the practices of using a Christmas tree to celebrate the birth of the Messiah and searching for Easter eggs are recent additions to the lives of Christians in the English-speaking world. There was even an intense debate about the use of the pipe organ for church music. Yet now, nothing is considered more "Christian" than the resounding melodies of Johann Sebastian Bach or George Frideric Handel's *Messiah*.

Even the much venerated rosary was introduced to the Western world by Islam; Muslims, in turn, got the idea of prayer beads from the Buddhists. Probably only God or the Buddha knows where it all began. Good ideas have a way of wandering around the world, even the religious world. My grandmother did not care where the first rosary came from; for her it marked the profound piety she felt for the Virgin Mary and the Roman Catholic tradition and faith. Besides, origins are less important than outcomes in most cases, as we have argued before. The Christian church began as a Jewish sect and spread to a wider world. At least from the Christian viewpoint, this growth was seen as a signal success.

The real question for today is not so much that syncretism or religious borrowing exists, but whether it is stable or correct. However, it is crucial to keep another query in mind. Is multiple religious participation as we have been describing it really the same thing as syncretism? Do Christians who add some Zen meditation to their lives intend to found a new religion? The answer is, Probably not. My hypothesis is that most people who cross the old boundaries of religious practice do not intend to move their membership from one community to another. If they do want to move, then they convert to the new religion. If they become convinced that Buddhism is the answer for them, they formally take refuge in the Buddha, the *dharma* (the teachings of the Buddha), and the *sangha* (the community founded by the Buddha). In other words, they become Buddhists.

This is a place to stop for a moment and ask ourselves, What in the world is going on here? I have come to believe that something very, very new, even revolutionary, is happening in the religious life of North America. Let me be clear. Something like multiple religious participation has happened in other parts of the world at other times, but this does not mean that it is not new in North America and probably Europe. It is something much beyond the New Age, though this is the movement that captures the most attention. My suspicion is that this kind of borrowing has been much more common than we think. But like the religious lives of women and minority people, it was considered unimportant if not a little bit suspect by organized, orthodox religious authorities.

However, all of this is changing for a host of reasons. First, there is the simple fact, as the German philosopher G. W. F. Hegel wrote in the nineteenth century, that when you tell people they are free, they begin to act as if they *are* free. What Hegel theorized was that the political and social emancipation flowing from the American and French revolutions was a mighty tide of personal and social emancipation in world history. Of course, the early fathers (and they were men) of these two revolutions were limited in their vision of who could be truly free. For instance, the framers of the American experiment in freedom did not see the necessity, even though some raised the issue, of the freedom of African Americans and Native peoples. Nor did these early revolutionaries understand that the message of universal freedom was heard by women as well as men.

By the end of the twentieth century it is now clear that real political, religious, social, cultural, and economic freedom is the right of every human person. What began as a philosophy and social revolution in the nineteenth century has become a struggle for universal liberation at the turn of the millennium. The voices of women and people of color can no longer be silenced either because they lack the education and the means to speak for themselves or because their voices are discounted as less important than those of white males. In Asia and Africa, women are expanding this list to include women beyond their own "dead Asian and African males." Freedom, including religious freedom to wander, is abroad in the world as never before, driven by the forces of modern travel and communication technology.

One hypothesis that should be tested is that women have been more willing to cross boundaries than their male companions. Men often have argued that this is because women are not interested in doctrinal questions of truth. However, as women gain their own intellectual voices, they scoff at yet another male conceit about their purported intellectual inferiority. If that is what men want to continue to believe, not even the empirical reality of accomplished women in all modern walks of life will dissuade men of the errors of their observations about female intelligence. Moreover, women's intelligence did not always reach the same conclusions about world mission as the male leadership. For instance, the modern historian of mission Dana Robert quotes the early-twentieth-century American missionary Welthy Honsinger: "I believe in a generous God, not one who was narrow and tyrannous. I was not going to China to convert, but to teach and—if so blessed—to bring Christianity with me by precept and example, offering my heritage to others" (Robert 1997, 294). Needless to say, the male missionary leaders did not appreciate Honsinger's views at all.

We need to ask ourselves, Why is it that women always play such an important role in the creation of new forms of religion? And then, once the success of their enterprise has become obvious to all, men rush in to take over and rewrite history in order to claim that they, the men, were always in the vanguard. None of this would have been news to the women around the Cross or at the empty tomb. It was these women who stayed the course with Jesus and not the men. However, it was men who began to push the women who had known and followed Jesus out of leadership in the early Jesus movement. Many of my women friends ask, So what else is new? When something is new and founded by women, men do not want anything to do with it. But once they see the success of a new religious movement, men assume that women cannot lead anything and are always willing to offer their organizational skills, for a price: the subservience of women.

Linked to the expanding role of women and people of color in the modern Christian world is the fact that Christians, for the most part, have become apostles of universal human rights. One of the key features of modern human rights theory is the fundamental freedom for each person to be in complete charge of his or her mind, heart, conscience, and faith. No one has the right to dictate personal religious choices for any other person. It is hard to emphasize how radical and novel this affirmation of religious freedom is. Christians have not always believed so. For instance, a Wiccan revival would have been unthinkable in Salem, Massachusetts, in the seventeenth century. The Puritans did not dialogue with or even tolerate witches; they executed them after the infamous witch trials. Women now note that most of those who suffered were women who held less than orthodox views from the perspective of the powerful male clergy.

The history of Christianity in the Western world after the collapse of the Pax Romana was often one of war and coercion. The chronicle of Charlemagne and forced conversion of the Saxons is a case in point at the beginning of medieval Europe. Slightly later, the church, as the Muslims discovered in the Crusades, was a warlike church. I do not recount these stories just to defame the history of the church; yet we must remember this violence in the name of religion if we are to move forward in conversation with the larger world. To wallow in guilt is counterproductive. To acknowledge the point and then release it in light of better knowledge of the world is what is needed. A Muslim friend has often pointed out to me that both Christianity and Islam have been more effective missionary religions when they were propagated by loving missioners, doctors, teachers, merchants, and wandering mystics rather than by the military arm of the state. My Buddhist friends joke with me that I am good at guilt. They point out that to know the truth, to recognize reality, is good; but then, you have to let go of the past as a form of grasping what cannot be grasped. Let it go and move on. Good advice.

But move on to where? To a pluralistic, changing, and relational world. Amid all the debates about the changes in modern religious life, some of the most fundamental transformations lie below the surface of the debates. The debates are about the doctrines and practices of new religions in the Western world, but the real issues have to do with our basic perceptions of the world itself. For instance, most people today believe in a world of change, process, transformation, relationships, and pluralism. This is very different from the worldview of the Protestant Reformation and even the Enlightenment. One of the outcomes of our changed worldview is that we now see religious intolerance as misguided as the support of slavery a century ago. This transformation is deeper even than many of our specific religious convictions, and it is now simply part of the way we see the world prior to the articulation of how religion fits into the new worldview.

To suggest that there is a deep operating system for our beliefs below even the basic operating system, something like a computer's BIOS (basic input-output system) that is even more embedded than DOS (Disk Operating System), Apple, or Windows, may seem somewhat recherché. How many of us, even the competent ones, have ever tried to change the BIOS of our computers? How many of us have even questioned its pivotal role as we change from program to program on our hard drives? Yet embedded worldviews drastically affect our religious beliefs. For instance, our modern scientific picture of the world is one of change, relationships, and forces that move and dance before our eyes. Biological species are born, die, and between life and death transform and migrate around the world. Moreover, the cosmos is now a vast place, so large and so old that we are not yet sure how old or how large. Most certainly the earth and its sun are no longer the center of creation; we are one blue spaceship spinning at the end of one arm of one galaxy. This is a very different world from the time of Jesus or the great medieval scholars and early modern reformers and counterreformers. The world is no longer flat and limited.

I will return to a major example of the impact of worldview on religion in chapter 6, where we will explore the topic of ecology. For instance, if we view nature as dead, as merely mechanical, as merely the random flux of subatomic particles and their forces, and we combine this with a reading of the Genesis account in the Bible that tells us to multiply and dominate the world, it is hard to think of nature as anything but a very large machine given by God for human use. Even on this reading of nature, it would be nice if we did not abuse the machine. What many ecologists argue is that we now know more about the living quality of the world around us, and that we need to realize that we are part of nature, not above nature as some kind of cosmic exception. Furthermore, we must learn reverence, as Albert Schweitzer wrote, for all life. This would be an example of a really fundamental worldview transformation.

Another way to look at this question of mixing different religions is to reflect on the African American theological experience. As I noted in the preface, African American scholars do not find the question of multiple religious experience nearly as problematic as do Euro-American theologians. The reason for this is that African Americans have always had to live in at least two different worlds. As a minority community they have had to negotiate with the larger community around them for their place in society; along with suffering the iniquity of racism, they have become bicultural. As a religious community African Americans are aware that many of the distinctive features of their present forms of theology, worship, and piety carry the imprint of the history of European forms of Christianity along with aspects of traditional African religions. While it is no longer easy to uncover all the African roots and branches of the African American church, there is an assurance among African American scholars that these roots and branches have helped shape the characteristic features of their traditions.

It is crucial to note that African American Christian scholars have no doubt that they belong to the Christian movement. Within the family of churches in North America no one questions the piety and socially committed faith of African Americans. The whole history of the modern civil rights movement and the theologies of Howard Thurman, Martin King Luther, Jr., James Cone, and Katie Cannon testify to the fact that a Christian can be evangelical and yet open to other peoples and religions. Nonetheless, African Americans also acknowledge that their faith includes their memories and contributions of ancestral traditions from beyond the European Christian world. When we talk about faithful endurance for the sake of the gospel, to suggest that the faith of African Americans is not stable sounds silly and insulting. But notice something else. All the diverse elements of African American Christian piety are definitively shaped by the Christian theological story.

Multiple religious participation is not essentially syncretism as some new religion. Even when crossing boundaries, or even when expanding boundaries, people do return home. Save for some eclectic followers of the New Age, few members of new religious movements understand themselves as creating something novel. Wiccans believe that they are reviving and refashioning the ancient nature religion of the European world for the contemporary ecological struggle. Of course, Wiccans believe other things as well, such as an appreciation of ritual, magic, and meditation. If the Buddhists in North America are masters of presenting meditation for laypeople, the Wiccans bring magic back into our lives. They are the magicians who provide the reenchantment of a world grown stale when seen only through the lens of a rigid scientism.

Multiple religious participation is the conscious (and sometimes even unconscious) use of religious ideas, practices, symbols, meditations, prayers, chants, and sensibilities derived from one tradition by a member of another community of faith for their own purposes. The example of the rosary is a perfect example because it is now so benign. It never would have occurred to my Roman Catholic grandmother that she was making use of a meditative-prayer technique originally found in Buddhism, transmitted to Islam, and then transplanted in the Latin West in the medieval world of the Crusades. I am not even sure that she would have found it interesting. It was simply part of her deep faith in her Lord and her Holy Church and its tradition. It was as Christian to my grandmother as was the Mass that she never missed for over thirty years, save for one visit to the hospital.

Let us return to our computer analogy for a moment. Every computer has a set of basic operating systems, its BIOS, that is often obscure even to a skilled user. These operating systems run all the other specialized programs that make the modern computer a household commodity. The fundamental religious commitment of a person (and maybe even a whole tradition) is like the fundamental operating system when it is linked to its more specialized operating system such as DOS or Windows. Although even the basic operating system is modified over time, it remains a specific system and not something else unless and until the BIOS is radically transformed. For instance, this is why people use either Apples or PCs. The distinction is drawn at the level of basic operating systems. But in order to change the whole system, sometimes even the BIOS must be updated for the computer to handle a new version of Windows (95, 98, and no doubt new ones into the next century), for instance.

The computer analogy can be pushed even further. At the beginning, the idea behind basic operating systems was not only to run the computer but to make sure that only Apple- or Microsoft-compliant programs could run with that computer. Over time computers and their operating systems have become more flexible. Nowadays a person can run programs across "platforms," as the computer wizards say. But the basic operating systems stay firmly in place. An Apple may be able to run your favorite Microsoft program, but it still runs it within an Apple universe. However, computer programmers have recognized that the day when people stay within the pristine realm of only one operating system is gone. If you want to deal with graphics, the Apple is still the best. But if you want to deal with huge gulps of data, then Microsoft database programs are the way to go.

Of course, the analogy can only be pushed so far. People and religions are not basic computer operating systems. Complicated questions of fidelity to family, tradition, self, and even God never enter the computer's algorithms. Nonetheless, and as process theologians such as A. N. Whitehead, Charles Hartshorne, and John B. Cobb, Jr., have ceaselessly been telling the theological community, the world never holds still. The Spirit of God blows where it will and creates new things. As Revelation teaches, Lo, all things are new. We could add the words *renewed* and *stimulated* to round out the equation of modern religious transformation. To pretend that nothing ever changes in any way is to run against one of the insights of the new processive and relational worldview emerging around the globe.

When a Christian makes use of a Buddhist form of centering meditation, she may, like my grandmother with her rosary, have no idea whatsoever that this is something from beyond her own religious world. But this is not always the case. In 1987, at an international Buddhist-Christian dialogue in Berkeley, California, I was taking part in a teaching and practice seminar on meditation taught by a Trappist monk. As he talked to us about how he worked with his own postulants, he told a complicated story of MRPing (remember, multiple religious participation). He had been a teacher of novices for years, and one of the things he did was to begin training them in the meditative arts. He had done this for decades and was a learned and conscientious practitioner of his trade.

Our Trappist teacher told us a few years before the seminar he had become involved in a joint visitation project with a great Tibetan exile monastery in India. Monks were invited to share in each other's practice and prayer. As the Trappist more closely observed the work of the Tibetan novice master, it became more and more clear to him that both the Tibetan monk and he were working at the same basic meditational task. They were both teaching their students how to calm the human mind. What the Trappist found challenging was that the Buddhist practice shortened the typical length of time that he needed, using his traditional Christian methods for imparting this basic kind of meditation. This led to a long conversation with his new Tibetan friend about what the Buddhist tradition was doing for its novice monks.

In the end the Trappist told us that he decided, with proper discussion with the other monks in his abbey, to try out the Buddhist methodology for centering meditation. The Trappist discovered that this basic teaching technique worked as well for his Christian students as it did for the young Buddhist novices. Our Trappist guide went on to tell us that he would not automatically try to copy other forms of Buddhist meditation. He explained that it appeared to him and his Buddhist friend that at the simpler levels of meditation, the question of what technique to use is religiously neutral. What he meant was that the technique of calming the mind worked just as well for a Christian as for a Buddhist when used within the larger matrix of Christian formation.

Our Trappist was very careful to point out that there were more advanced forms of meditation and prayer that could not be used across religious boundaries. He explained that this was because content and method could not always be so easily interwoven. For instance, there really was a difference between meditation on the gracious works and teachings of the Virgin Mary for the Christian and for the compassionate White Tara for the Buddhist. At a certain level of specificity, the Buddhist and the Christian teacher were clear that the differences in tradition mattered for the believer. Respect for the other tradition could and should always be there, and even reverent participation was appropriate from time to time. But there are simply some prayers and practices, such as the Mass, that would not be appropriate for a Buddhist to participate in, and vice versa for the Christian. In this early period of Buddhist-Christian dialogue, each one of these practices needed to be examined carefully on a case-by-case basis in order to discover its interreligious portability. The key for the monks was a fundamental respect for the religious life of their communities and for the individuals in their spiritual care.

My general observations (completely unscientific if extensive in space and time) led me to conclude that MRPing is more like adding new programs to our religious computer than tinkering with the basic operating system. An example from the religious history of China makes the point. In the sixteenth and seventeenth centuries in China there was a movement known as "the three religions are one." In this case, the religions being conjoined were Confucianism, Buddhism, and Taoism. What this meant was that some religious leaders argued that these three great religions were actually one manifestation of the divine reality at the most basic spiritual level even if their surface teachings were highly differentiated. Both the basic unity and the mundane diversity were celebrated. Part of the argument was that each tradition took care of different aspects of human life. For instance, Taoists and Buddhists were much better at the life of meditation, whereas Confucians were more skilled at running government bureaucracies in a just and harmonious fashion. Everyone agreed that all three traditions, being Chinese, taught respect for elders and fundamental filial piety.

Scholars often assumed that this movement was syncretistic. However, I believe that it was more eclectic than syncretistic. By this I mean that when you look carefully at these diverse early modern Chinese thinkers you discover very strong root systems at the base of what can be a very wild looking tree, to switch from a computer to a tree metaphor. Olive trees, for instance, were favorites of Jesus and the early Christian movement when they wanted to make a point about moving across ethnic and communal boundaries. In the tree you can find grafts of all kinds generating new branches, but nonetheless it is clear that you have a Taoist, Confucian, or Buddhist taproot that nourishes the olive tree.

There was nothing duplicitous about what these Chinese masters were doing. They lived in a religious world that condoned and appreciated borrowing across traditional boundaries. If another tradition had a good idea, then use it. In this regard, the various traditions were individually stimulated and strengthened by fertilizer and new grafts from another tradition. No new grand traditions emerged. In many respects, we are now living in a world much more like that of these early modern Chinese masters than we are in the world of medieval Christian isolation from daily and significant contact with people of other faiths.

I have come to believe that modern MRPers seek to enrich and renew, but not to replace, the fundamentals of root religion. Of course, not many people who have multiple practices even think about them in these complex historical and theological terms. They simply go about their religious lives within their primary community of faith. However, this raises the question of how to understand formal membership in any religion in a pluralistic age. This question is as complicated as the practices themselves.

In coming to terms with questions of formal membership in religious institutions, history is again a valuable guide to theory and practice. Not all religions have interpreted membership, participation, or adherence in the same way. That is not surprising given the vast range of ways that religions have organized themselves. There are some traditions to which you belong because of birth. Judaism, Shinto, aboriginal traditions, and Hinduism are good examples of historic religions that define membership in terms of birth within a specific community. In fact, Jewish and Hindu friends have explained to me that "being religious" or "observant" has little or nothing to do with formal membership or recognition within their communities. There are even whole schools of quite orthodox Hindu philosophy that are resolutely atheistic. Some Hindu schools reject the cogency and efficacy of any belief in God. There are also Jews for whom the tradition is a culture that merely happens to have a religious dimension. However odd this understanding seems to other Jews and Hindus, none would deny membership in the community to people born within the fold of the faith. Another example of this understanding of membership would be the primal or indigenous traditions all over the world. You are a Cheyenne because you are born one and not because you seek any kind of formal membership or conversion to the tribal religion, language, and culture.

But you are not born a Christian; you are baptized one. Muslims say that we are all born Muslims, but that we must affirm our own participation in the Islamic way for ourselves. Christianity and Islam have the strictest understandings of what it means to be a member of their tradition in terms of consciously joining the faith as opposed to merely being born into it. Of course, Judaism has accepted sincere converts even though it definitely is not a missionary tradition like Christianity or Islam (at least since the Greco-Roman world).

The early Jesus movement, which began as a Jewish sect, learned to define itself over against its parent. Later Christians continued this family debate with the new revelation of Islam; sibling rivalry flowered between these two daughter traditions of Israel. And as with so many family quarrels, the debate about how a person was to be counted as in or out of what movement flared into open and ongoing conflict. For instance, there is a group called Jews for Jesus that claims to be Jewish followers of Jesus; the movement makes use of many traditional forms of Jewish prayer, worship, and culture. Jews, given the history of Jewish-Christian relations, are dubious about such claims and consider the movement merely another example of evangelical Christians deviously seeking to convert unwary Jews.

Quite early in the development of the related yet more and more distant early gentile church and Judaism in the first and second centuries, the debate between the Jesus movement and its Jewish parents became so heated that a fundamental decision was made that a person could not be both a Jew and a Christian at the same time. You could be one or the other, but not both. Later the Muslim position on membership was the same. Although Muslims are enjoined to respect the other "People of the Book," meaning Jews, Christians, and a few other specific traditions, one cannot be a follower of Islam and remain a Christian or a Jew.

The theological solution offered by Islam is called supersessionism. This means that the newer religion believes that it either reforms, perfects, or replaces the older traditions. The newer religion says that the older traditions were fine as far as they went, but they have now been surpassed by a new or renewed revelation. The apologetic logic is that if you are truly a good Jew or Christian, you will see, with a clear and open conscience, that the teachings of Islam conform to the best of your old tradition and in fact perfect what had become a corrupted version of the truth. Of course, this is exactly the same argument that Christians used for centuries on Jews. Needless to say, such arguments have engendered intense debate and even fratricidal conflict for hundreds of years between the three religions that claim Abraham and Sarah as their common ancestors.

In Asia the situation was and is distinct. The linked cultures of China, Korea, Japan, and Vietnam see the question of membership in religious institutions differently. It is not considered odd in any of these cultures for people to claim, quite sincerely and with a great deal of thought, that they are members of more than one religion. This is not really a case of syncretism in the sense that there is a conscious effort to create new religions, though that does happen from time to time. Rather, someone who is a Confucian is convinced that both Taoism and Buddhism have something profound to add to her life. As some modern Confucians have told me, they believe that Buddhism has a wonderful system of meditation and that Taoists have a refined sense of the beauty of nature along with a wonderful sense of humor. They believe that as Confucians they would be foolish not to incorporate these elements into Confucian practice. I have had Buddhist colleagues tell me much the same thing about their feelings toward Confucianism and Taoism. There is mutual appreciation but not a lack of identity or even conviction.

Religious identity and conviction are key elements in this equation. A person's sense of self-identity ranks each of the religions in terms of what they mean for his or her self-definition. But what do we mean by ranking? Does this mean that a sincere person must say that one religion is better than another? This is not how the issue is discussed in East Asia. The characteristic way is to affirm the mutual worth of each tradition. Rather than ranking each by means of some kind of logical truth-value, it is recognized that there is a correlative or complementary nature between and among religious traditions. Just as each person has certain talents, each religion does some things better than the others do. Therefore, accidents of birth and inclination are crucial for a person's sense of religious choice and identity. From the East Asian perspective, religions complement each other in the cultivation of human flourishing and proper relationship to divine things. The divine reality is clever enough to provide a whole feast of teachings for persistently dull humanity.

The East Asian way of looking at the world is a difficult one for many Jews, Christians, and Muslims. We children of Abraham and Sarah have been nurtured to believe that our particular path is the correct one. Or in the Jewish case, Judaism is normative for Jews and not for others. The classical Jewish position on the religion of other people is that if the righteous gentiles are faithful to the fundamentals of religious life as they have been taught by the one true God, then they too will have a just portion of the Kingdom to come. Christians and Muslims have believed that their tradition commands them to be less generous to others. It is the task of Christians and Muslims to bring the truth of their specific traditions to all other peoples.

While many modern Christians and Muslims have become more tolerant of people of other faiths, there is still the lingering doubt about the place of other religions in God's final scheme for universal human redemption. All other traditions, however worthy they may be, are unstable as to their final goal; from the Christian perspective, at the end of time the sincere Hindu will come to realize that his Lord is none other than Jesus as the Christ. Other religions either will not get you to heaven or once you are in heaven, you will then learn the error of your ways and finally see the truth of God's teaching in the incarnation of Jesus of Nazareth and the tradition of the Church Universal and Militant.

Here again, the East Asian (and South Asian) view is generally different. It is based more on the specifics of the individual's religious needs and social location than on the generality of one cosmic religious plan. In short, one size does not fit all. Each person, according to Buddhist, Confucian, and Taoist sensibilities, is different. To follow the specific Confucian path, the argument is that each of us has a specific endowment that we receive from heaven. It is up to us to cultivate this endowment as best we can; Confucianism recognizes that very few of us can cultivate our human nature successfully on our own. The Confucian tradition is profoundly communal in character. Each one of us needs our family, our friends, our teachers, our colleagues, and our religious tradition in order to have a chance to cultivate ourselves successfully. Only a true sage can practice self-cultivation without too much assistance, and even Confucius never claimed to be a sage or to have encountered a sage in his lifetime.

However, from the Confucian viewpoint, we are not left completely to our own devices. Confucius was sure that there were sages in the past because he had access to their writings, the classics of his tradition. He pointed out that these classics, as the historical records of the sages, provide us with suitable road signs for our own cultivation. If you want to check your progress in cultivating virtue, see if your passions, thoughts, and deeds conform to the model provided by the ancient sages. You should make frequent use of the Confucian classics and teachers on your way to humaneness. If you manage to match the instructions of the sages, you are on the path to the Confucian Way.

Of course, one of the marks of traveling the Confucian Way is a growing ethical and intellectual humility that makes you realize that try as hard as you might to conform to the model of the sages, there is always more for you to do. As Confucius taught his best student, Yen Hui, the road is long and the burden is heavy. Moreover, just when you think you have reached your destination, you discover that in reaching your first goal the sages are already providing you with yet another goal to seek; the process never ends until death. The path is endless but not joyless. The joy is in following the path itself, in knowing that you are trying to do the best you can.

Confucius, as did numerous Taoist and Buddhist teachers over the centuries, tailored his teachings to the capacities of his students. For the brave and perhaps rash young warrior, Confucius counseled prudence; for the timid and retiring scholar, he urged more forceful action in support of justice. Later East Asian thinkers argued that each religious tradition was like a special kind of medicine. Each one of us needs a different medicine from time to time. However, the traditions of East Asia also argued for the fact that each of us needs to commit ourselves to a coherent spiritual path. In this regard, the tested wisdom of the race suggests that each of us needs to choose a specific path and follow it with true integrity. Nonetheless, there was nothing wrong with keeping one's eyes open for other good suggestions from other doctors of the soul.

Although it is too early to say, I profoundly believe that Westerners can learn a great deal from the East Asian perspective on multiple religious participation. In one sense it is simply empirically and historically true. People do borrow from each other across religious boundaries all the time. The problem has been that in the West this was often seen as a bad thing for the most part. The Christian faith was believed to be complete and definitive for all times and places. However, this reading of religious history runs counter to the modern observation of the changing nature of human life and history. We have learned that the world is vaster than we thought in the ancient, medieval, and Reformation worlds. Besides the world's being physically and culturally vast and diverse, one of the teachings of modern science, whether natural, social, or historical, is that things change over time. The world is in a constant process of creative transformation and synthesis. Of course there are things that endure. But one of the marks of the living is suppleness and receptivity, not being hard, unyielding, and unreceptive. At an elementary level, if we did not eat new things every day, we would soon die.

If the move to an East Asian model is too difficult to contemplate, we can think of a second reason to learn to appreciate the MRP factor in human religious history. In the Jewish and Christian streams of this history, humankind is given a list of ten moral and religious commandments to follow. One commandment is not to bear false witness against the neighbor. This injunction now has a global reach. Our sense of who the neighbor is has been expanded beyond our home communities to take in the whole world as it comes to us on the international evening news or in our morning paper. What happens in Bosnia and Kosovo and the economic ups and downs in Bangkok and Tokyo impact the price of autos down the street.

How can we be faithful to the commandment not to bear false witness against our neighbors if we know nothing about their religion? This is not just a question about secular education. As we look at the world at the end of the Cold War and the beginning not only of a new century but also of a new millennium, we are struck by the resurgence of religion around the world. Moreover, it is crystal-clear that religions continue to define who and what we are as moral or immoral beings. As the international political analyst Samuel Huntington writes, the fault lines of crisis and conflict run now between the great civilizations of the world, and these civilizations are defined by their religions more than anything else, at least when they begin to think about their identities. Religion does more to define civilization than does language, location, or race.

As the contemporary theologian Hans Küng has argued, if there is ever going to be peace in the world, there must be peace between and among religions. And if there is going to be peace between and among religions, there must be understanding between and among religious people. Understanding does not mean bland agreement. But it does mean learning about the other. Following the lead of East Asian religions, we must all learn to learn from each other.

Chapter 3

Where Is *the* Truth Blended in the Pudding?

Among many other claims, most religions maintain that they are true, meaning that they tell the truth about reality and the way to salvation, paradise, union with the divine or nirvana. Along with these basic truth claims trail other primal virtues such as insight into the good, beautiful, liberating, loving, sustaining, saving, and humane. By these means religions provide a way to put a flawed person right with the divine reality. But then, what is the truth? As all Christians know, Pontius Pilate in the Gospels was not just asking a disinterested question about Jewish religious and theological concerns; as a Roman governor, Pilate had the responsibility to preserve public order and maintain Roman authority in Jerusalem. We must remember that this was a tense time of political conflict in the restive land of the Jewish people. There was an interweaving of definition (propositions about who was or was not the King of the Jews), action (the arrest and trial of a young Jewish religious leader), and exhibition of various worldviews in conflict (the passion of Jesus of Nazareth). The Jewish leaders desired one outcome, the Roman authorities another, and Christians have now spent almost two thousand years trying to ascertain just what Jesus was doing in this cosmic drama.

Another less dramatic anecdote is in order here. Unlike some of my other stories, this one has little cosmic significance. When I accompanied my parents to Hong Kong in the fall of 1964 as a visiting undergraduate at the University of Hong Kong, none of us had ever been to any part of East Asia, much less studied anything about Chinese culture. Early in our stay we were invited to attend the marriage of a young Chinese friend. I can't remember why we were going to send flowers to one of the events leading up to the ceremony, but we were. The flowers were white. Another Chinese friend was in the apartment before we sent the flowers off, and although he opined that they were beautiful, he warned us that they were the wrong color entirely for a festive marriage. He told us that white in Chinese culture is the color of mourning and bereavement and that it would be insensitive to send such flowers to the young couple. My mother and father were aghast and thanked our friend profusely for saving them from making such an intercultural social gaffe.

Where was truth in this aborted giving of white flowers for a wedding? Were the flowers true or untrue? Was the color true or untrue? Was our friend's advice true or untrue? Most people will answer that the only place truth enters is with the last question, namely, that our friend told us the truth about the Chinese religious and cultural world, saving our family great embarrassment. Our question in this chapter is, Can we talk about multiple religious participation sensibly in terms of truth? Is the truth of religion something like the colors of social convention and intercultural good manners?

The easy counterquestion is (and this is what Pilate, like any sensible official faced with a tough question, did) to play for time and ask, What do you mean by the truth? The history of Western philosophy is littered with diverse theories about the nature of truth. There is the truth of coherence (that the world coheres in a fundamental way such that all true statements fit together logically), of correspondence (that a true statement corresponds to the way things really are), or of pragmatic truth (if it works it is true). Religions often give a special twist to the question of truth and suggest that truth is a matter of persons, of their integrity, their piety, and their faith. Of course, for monotheists the greatest person, if you can use that language, is the creator God, architect, sustainer, and redeemer

of all creation. Plato, toward the beginning of the Western philosophic venture, suggested that the three highest things a person could
contemplate were the true, the good, and the beautiful. Plato went
on to argue that the real measure of civilization was the victory of
persuasion over force. In the garden before his final passion, Jesus
embodied Plato's theoretical insight into the power of truth as persuasion. Furthermore, Jesus is reported to have told his followers that
the truth would set them free.

What follows will be the most philosophically complex part of
the book. I apologize to those readers who lack any taste for such
intricate intellectual spiderwork. However, I believe that it is necessary because it lies at the core of an absolutely crucial issue. This is
the conundrum of "what does it all matter," the so what if there are
many religions and people wander around among them searching for
truth. Isn't it the case that truth is merely in the eye of the believer? If
we discover, as we have already, that people have different views of
reality and that different religions are all worthy of our respect, then
why bother to believe anything at all? Edward Gibbon, the great
historian of the Roman Empire, wrote that a refined and cynical
Roman bureaucrat believed that all religions were equally useful in
controlling the public and equally false in terms of defining the way
the world really is. Why should we believe anything if we live in such
a radically pluralistic world? This is ultimately a question of truth, of
where we put our faith, or where we take a stand, and how we understand the plausibility conditions of our common world.

Philosophers have the luxury of doubt; Pontius Pilate did not because he had to adjudicate justice (or the Roman imperial law) in an
all-too-real world of politics and enflamed religious debate. But even
the great David Hume, perhaps the most famous doubter of the modern world, when he arose from his philosophic speculations, returned
to his billiard table with the firm belief that a good bank shot would
land the three ball in the side pocket. In short, Hume's beliefs about
the world allowed him to act in it with certainty in some areas, such
as parlor games, if not in the domain of the final foundations of
truth. People need a set of warranted beliefs about themselves and

the world in order to function in any civilized sense. If they do not have such shared assumptions, they can, of course, practice barbarism, the domination of the young, strong, and clever over everyone else. They can become Nazis; but this is not what most people want even if they are seduced by the immediate appeals of barbarism to solve some complicated social problem immediately.

Questions of truth are deep ones indeed. They are intimately linked to our ways of viewing the world. If we think that we know the world, then we will frame propositions about it in accordance with our worldviews. For instance, few people continue to believe that the moon is made of blue cheese after the moon landings of the past few decades. In fact, given the modern scientific worldview of the preceding three centuries, I seriously doubt that many people held out for a new supply of Stilton cheese even before the first astronauts landed on the moon in 1969. Our view of the world does not allow for the notion that the moon is made of cheese.

Nonetheless, most truly religious people believe that their faith commitments and their worldviews are unified. This has been the case in the past and is so now for many people. However, there are periods of historical transformation when the old beliefs (both religious and secular) were and are challenged by new ways of looking at the world. For instance, if we are living in a world where we are more conscious of the changing nature of reality and its intricate web of relationships (modern feminism, ecology, management theory, and systems analysis all agree on this new worldview), then we are in the midst of a "change" of worldviews. We are moving from a mechanical to a processive, relational view of reality. We shall return to this question more fully in chapter 6, when we look at the ecological crisis.

Worldviews are the lenses we use to look at a world in a certain way. It does matter if you have corrective lenses, sunglasses, or bifocals. They frame our understanding of science, religion, the political order, the economy, and technology. They define what we take to be good arguments and the warrants for any proof that we might have about disputed facts. Worldviews both focus and narrow what we take to be reality; we no longer believe the world is flat and this means that no explorer now looks for an edge to the world, or perhaps even the universe itself. One of the great instances of this kind of worldview debate concerns the account of creation as told by modern science and the alternative conservative Christian view based on a particular reading of the Bible's version of creation. The expositions are different, but the worldview power of "science" is so strong that even the Christians who continue to dislike Darwin and the theory of evolution are forced to call their rival vision of reality "Creation Science." They claim that, along with its other merits, the Bible is also a sound book of science. Needless to say, secular and more liberal Christian scientists have a hard time recognizing anything like their view of science in this appeal to biblical truth. Yet both religious theories are governed by a worldview that acknowledges the power of modern science and technology rather than the details of biblical scholarship.

One of the problems with looking at multiple religious participation is that we have a vague intuition about the nature of truth that is curiously truncated in light of the breadth of human religious experience. Chuang Tzu, the most brilliant of the early Chinese Taoists, argued that most of us clutch one corner of the truth and proclaim it the whole truth. It is rather, Chuang Tzu said, like chatting with a frog who, sitting comfortably in his well, maintains stoutly that the sky is a small blue circle. This is a great definition for the frog based on his experience; generations of Chinese, Koreans, Japanese, Vietnamese, and now North Americans have been amused and instructed by Chuang Tzu's little parable about the dangers of all-too-facile generalization when seeking the truth.

Theologians and philosophers have noticed that many people, when pressed to define truth, do so by asserting that matters of truth have to do with propositional statements about reality. Only assertions qua propositions are truthful. It is either snowing or it is not, and these kinds of assertive propositions can be tested empirically or logically or both, especially if the stuff falling in January in Boston is cold, flaky, and white. Assertions are made in terms of language.

Hence, assertive propositions are the only proper warrants of truth claims. The problem is that language is conventional (and often ambiguous), as the Red Queen taught Alice in Wonderland. However, just because language is conventional, this does not mean that it is always imprecise. Try telling a local judge that you, based on your sudden realization of the conventional reality of traffic signs, decided that the red light really meant "go" even though it meant "stop" to the misguided police officer who arrested you. The truth would not be in doubt in any serious way in this exchange before the traffic court.

Along with assertive propositions about truth, the contemporary American philosopher Justus Buchler suggested that there are two other forms of truth claims that run parallel to those of propositions. The first is what he calls the exhibitive, and this is most often illustrated by aesthetic claims about beauty. Is it fair to say that a wonderful painting like Rembrandt's *Nightwatch* is true? Yet the huge canvas in Amsterdam surely exhibits something profoundly true about human nature and the community of Dutch burghers gathered to protect their liberty and way of life in the seventeenth century. Or when we look at a Chinese Sung dynasty (960–1279) landscape painting, can we say that these swirling mountains and streams are true? Of course, there are no landscapes that look just like a Chinese landscape painting, even in the wonderfully water-carved karst topography of South China.

In fact, we would probably think it an odd thing to ask, Is this Chinese landscape hanging scroll true? Yet there is something true and beautiful about it. It is a work of surpassing artistic achievement. Furthermore, with its depiction of a tiny human traveler almost lost in the midst of the swirling clouds passing through the mountains, streams, lakes, and forests, it does tell us about our lives as human beings set in the wider canvas of the cosmos. Is this insight into our relation to nature true? It isn't even a proposition. Sometimes you have to squint at the scroll to see the tiny human figure wandering in the beauty of the imagined landscape. Nevertheless we claim that one picture is worth a thousand words. The landscape tells us that we are one part of a much vaster and beautiful world.

Buchler then adds a third domain for truth: What about actions? Can we call them true? In some cases this is just what we do. Many Quakers, Confucians, Gandhians, and African American civil rights leaders learned the art of speaking truth to power. Philosophers have even noticed a whole range of verbal statements they call performative utterances. A classic example of a performative utterance is a marriage vow. When the bride or groom says "I do," is this true? One can only hope so, but to say "I do" does not in and of itself express any formal truth claim comparable to noting that it is snowing on the wedding day. Yet when we think about the wedding, the young couple are making a truth claim about their commitment to each other and their changed legal standing in the community. Again, my local Boston judge would take this to be the case after reviewing the marriage documents.

Buchler argued that we must think of human communication in terms of assertive/propositional, exhibitive, and active modes of discourse. Sometimes these modes overlap. Here is a story from the Islamic world that illustrates the mixed nature of truth in the real world, or at least a fictional world. A woman is confronted in her home by a madman bent on killing her husband. The madman demands to know if her husband is at home. Anyone who has studied Western philosophy will immediately think of Immanuel Kant's categorical ethics. Kant argued that it is never proper to lie, even when confronted with a life-or-death situation. Kant's main point was that we should always act such that we could recommend any of our actions to anyone else and that our ethical maxims could become universal rules of conduct. Hence, you should never tell a lie, even to a madman.

When I teach about Kant this always strikes my students as a difficult case, even when they are perfectly clear that the woman should not tell the madman the whereabouts of her husband. The Muslim husband, who is at home and does not want to confront the madman, suggests a solution to the dilemma. He asks his wife to draw a circle on the floor of their house right in front of the door, and then to put her finger in that specific place and say, No, my husband is not here (of course, it is literally true that her husband is not in the little circle on the floor in front of the woman). The madman interprets this to mean that the husband is not in the house and leaves. In a formal sense, the woman has not lied to the madman; she has only told him a truth about a very small part of the house.

So what about taking part in someone else's religious ceremonies? How does this relate to being a truthful or faithful person? Actually, we take part in other people's celebrations all the time, I suspect. For instance, very few North Americans would think it odd to attend the wedding of a couple outside their own faith. However, in many traditions this means that we have participated in a religious ritual from another tradition. And if we as Christians invite a Jewish, Buddhist, Hindu, or Muslim friend to a wedding in our family, they too will be MRPing.

Some Jesuits in India have given this quite a bit of thought. They wanted to develop a rough-and-ready guide for the possibility of taking part in various Hindu religious ceremonies when invited to do so. Weddings were no problem for them, but other ceremonies were trickier. In the end they told me that they decided on one rule. They were happy to take part in any ceremony or festivity that did not demand that they become a formal part of that community. That is to say, they would decline the invitation to take part in a formal initiation ceremony or ritual. They also extended this to mean that they would not take part in any ceremony or festival that would imply to others that they were part and parcel of the Hindu community.

To explain what they meant, my Jesuit colleagues used the following analogy drawn from the Christian tradition. What if a Hindu colleague was moved by seeing Holy Communion and asked to participate in the sacred rite? My Jesuit friends said that they would have to say no, because from their point of view, to take part in the Communion would mean, at least tacitly, that the person was becoming part of the Christian community. Now, if the person was so moved by Holy Communion that they decided to convert to the Christian faith, that was another matter. However, the Jesuits believed that the Mass and Communion were so central to Christian self-understanding that it was inappropriate for a non-Christian to partake until conversion. However, the Jesuits were also clear that it was perfectly fine for a Hindu to attend a Christian worship service and profit from the sermon, prayers, and liturgy.

Another example. I have been invited to attend prayers at mosques from time to time. I asked a Muslim scholar if he thought that I could take part in the communal prayers that are so much a part of Muslim piety. He suggested that this was not appropriate for the same reason given by the Jesuit theologians. For me to take part in the prayers would indicate that I was part of the Muslim family. This would be confusing and disruptive to everyone, even though God would certainly understand my intentions to worship God. His suggestion was that I should simply observe the collective prayers reverently from the back of the room or just outside of the main prayer room if possible. Of course, my Muslim friend said that I could pray as a Christian if I were so moved. He was of the unshakable opinion that all pious prayers were welcomed by God.

These myriad encounters have convinced me that the question of truth in religious matters is a highly complicated one. Of course, there are times when the truth is clear. Having talked about Muslim prayer, let me tell another, less happy story. When I was working in Toronto, I would often be asked about how to deal with delicate questions of religious practice. Although I was an expert on very few of these matters, I developed a large phone list of friends that I could call for immediate advice. One afternoon I received a call from the Toronto police.

The police had just been alerted to a case of terrible sexual abuse. Someone had told them that a recently widowed young woman was being repeatedly raped by members of her deceased husband's family. When the police intervened and were in the process of rescuing the young woman and arresting the men involved, some of the men made the astounding claim that they were Muslims and simply following the common practice of their faith. Needless to say, this sounded strange to the officers, but they decided to call me to find out what I might know about the matter. I told them immediately that it sounded as bizarre to me as it did to them, but that I would call my Muslim colleagues immediately.

I made the calls, and two leading members of the Muslim community, a learned professor of religious studies and a local imam, responded as soon as they got the call. They were outraged that anyone would make such a claim about the Muslim tradition. They accompanied the police to set things right and to comfort the young woman. Later we had a chance to talk about the event. They were outraged that these men tried to cover their heinous acts, the rape of a distraught young widow, by making a false claim about Islamic teachings.

We all agreed that it was providential that I had been called by the police. However, both men found it terribly sad that anyone would have thought even for an instant that such a perversion of humane conduct could have been taught by the Muslim community. How could anyone believe such a falsehood? They went on to say that this demonstrated the need for more dialogue between Muslims and their neighbors about the true nature of Islam as a teaching of profound peace. It was clear to all of us that there was no truth at all in the claims of these perverted men. Nor was there any room for polite dialogue. The only response was swift police intervention and a clarion call for repentance, justice, and healing for the violated young woman.

These cases are clear. But others, alas, are less clear. This is where Buchler's list of three forms of human meaning is valuable. Again, the three are assertive (that is to say, propositions or statements of putative fact); exhibitive (such as in art or sports when we talk about the beauty of a perfectly executed fast break in basketball); and active (such as when we make a solemn promise of marriage, when the words themselves point to a bond of affection that is not merely a proposition about abstract belief). According to Buchler, not all truth claims are simply assertions of propositions. In fact, it would be very strange if they were because human beings do so much more with their lives than merely stand around constructing propositional strings of truth claims. They also have to do with acts and exhibitions. We play sports, create great art, write outrageous novels, get married, declare war, and bury our dead.

This dramatic range of human meaning making is obscured because religions, like philosophy, often rest solidly on textual foundations. Most of the great traditions have collected sacred writings. These great collections of writings are known as scripture and are construed as containing the essence of the particular thought and revelation of each cumulative tradition. Even when there is little or no appeal, such as in Buddhism or Confucianism, to divine origins for the texts, there is still the strong inclination to check present experience against the wise witness of previous ages. Scriptures provide a keel for most religions in that they act as a set of criteria to be used to evaluate words, deeds, actions, rituals, philosophies, worldviews, theologies, and meditations. Just as boats need a keel for ocean storms, so too do human beings need wise words in order to navigate the tempests of life's demands and pleasures. Scriptures occupy privileged positions because of their written, tangible, and permanent format; like keels, they offer stability within the whirlwind.

Of course, not all traditions have extensive sets of scriptures. Many primal or aboriginal religions do not have written scriptures at all. Yet one of the things that elders need to know is the history and narrative of their tradition. Without tradition there is nothing to pass on. Anyone who has been privileged to spend time listening to elders understands the profound depth of their learning and insight. Although scriptures are important for religions, the mere fact of writing, translation, and printing does not make a story a scripture.

Nonetheless, I know of no tradition that teaches that merely memorizing a list of dogmas will save, awaken, release, transform, enlighten, or liberate a person. For instance, the Christian tradition tells us that simply calling out the name of the Lord will not save anyone. Faith and prayer are good, but they must become alive in the world or they are merely verbal displays of fictional piety. My college students are brilliant critics of such protestations of true faith on the part of their parents. Rather, it is the quality of the embodied life, the true, active faith that saves; or rather, it is the mercy and love of God that inform sincere faith that saves even "a wretch like me." The great family of Pure Land Buddhist schools also teaches that it is the magnificent power of the universal compassionate vow of Amida Buddha that will save the lost and confused worldling from being locked into the endless realm of craving and suffering.

In fact, it is the case that religions inevitably speak about quality of life when they talk about the perfected person. This means that a person who becomes a saint or sage is remarkably different from the rest of us ordinary human beings. At one end of the spectrum we find Theravadin or Southern Buddhists and Confucians holding out for the necessity of ceaseless effort on the part of the person in order to achieve sageliness or the final peace of nirvana. No one can make you a Buddha or a Confucian sage save yourself, and that through profound effort. Of course, the final goal is quite different for the Buddhist and the Confucian. The Buddhist seeks awakening to reality as it is in order to obtain the release that eventuates in nirvana, escaping from the trammels of rebirth. The Confucian sage seeks to embody the Tao as the way of ethical and intellectual perfection in order to be of service to self and society.

At the other end of the spectrum are traditions such as Protestant (both liberal and evangelical) Christianity, Islam, and Pure Land Buddhism that stress the need for grateful faith in the saving power of a compassionate God or the Primal Vow of Amida Buddha. It is not the person who achieves salvation through works, but rather the humble soul that cries out to God or the Buddha for mercy. Of course, it does not hurt to try to lead an ethical, pious, and learned life either. But real wisdom is a gift of God's bounty or the dual wings of the Buddha's wisdom and compassion.

One of the main reasons why questions of truth are so difficult to capture in religious matters is that they are so humanly complicated, even without involving God or reality as such in claiming to solve the question of truth. I have stressed the human side of the reception; as difficult as it is to speak for one human being, think how hard it is to speak for all humanity, much less God. It is difficult enough to get simple propositions lined up to affirm truth-values in mathematics and logic where the beauty of order and precision reigns supreme. The problem is multiplied when a living, sensing, feeling, and socially interacting person is involved. Aristotle, toward the beginning of the Western intellectual tradition, taught that we should not seek for more precision than we can find in a subject matter. Truth (with a small *t*) is comparatively easy to recognize in simple situations where there are not very many elements to consider or variables to manipulate or where the ethical pattern is perfectly clear. The problem is that ethical situations only appear ethically transparent when there is unity within the community. Such unity is rare even within homogeneous religious traditions. In order to remind ourselves how difficult this is, all we need to do is observe the great debates that are raging within Protestant denominations about the role of homosexuals in the life of the churches in the last decades of the twentieth century. In a pluralistic setting the appeals of a common understanding of ethics or community standards of taste fade rapidly. The critics wonder, If anything goes in the name of art or lifestyles, can the same kind of indifferent concern for religious truth be far behind?

Theoretically and empirically, why should we assume that the search for truth is simple when complicated creatures such as human beings are involved? None of this clarity holds for individual persons when confronted by difficult ethical questions such as abortion or female genital mutilation. We also need to bear in mind that many (if not most) religions deal with more than the conduct and faith of a specific person but maintain that true religion is a corporate practice of many people, and perhaps even many generations over time.

As we have already seen, there are a number of appealing ways of trying to deal with the question of truth. One inviting formulation is to hold that this is not a proper question for human beings as finite creatures to raise. This is actually the classic Calvinist theory that the finite cannot encompass the infinite. However, the problem is that religions make profound claims on their adherents; religions enjoin us to at least obey, if not understand completely, the divine will. Why would one bother to be religious if the religion were not true? Furthermore, religions do assert that they hold the key to ultimate human salvation, liberation, or transformation.

There have been a number of theologians who argue that the best we can hope for is a relatively absolute form of truth. Somehow this sounds odd, even when it is said in complete sincerity based on good reasons. The reasons are almost always ethical in nature. Historians of religion, having reviewed the role that religions have played in various conflicts around the world over the centuries, draw the conclusion, and rightly so, that religious people are as warlike as anyone else, and perhaps even more so when they are convinced that God is on their side. The ethicists reason that if we can convince people that God is only on the side of those innocents who suffer during conflict, then we will have a chance to defuse the religious roots of conflict.

Nonetheless, religions do deal with ultimate things. It is almost impossible to isolate their claims about reality from claims about truth. However, the question is really even trickier than it seems. What if we refocus the issue on the relative nature of truth and not the relative nature of the divine reality? Can we believe that our religion is true because it is focused on the divine reality without believing that this means that we personally know its truth in all its fullness? I often tell my classes that I hope God is clever enough to save a sinner like me. Here again, there is something of a biblical warrant when Jesus reminds his eager disciples that only God is perfectly good. It is amusing how frequently the disciples fail to understand a slightly exasperated Jesus. At least one inference is that not even Jesus makes the claim for perfect goodness in a sense equal to the full divinity of God's complete majesty. On the other side of the world, Confucius never claimed to a sage. In fact, the only thing Confucius would claim for himself is that he knew no one who loved to learn from others more than he did.

Nor should we forget the most haunting question of the New Testament, namely, what is the truth? It is deceptively simple to assume that we know what we mean by truth when we live within a specific religious tradition, but perhaps that certitude is part of the problem when we grapple with the interaction of different religious practices. For instance, take the sentence "The wind is blowing the ashes." This could mean a number of things. It could mean that we are standing on the edge of a small forest and notice that the wind has come up and is blowing through the ash trees. Or it could mean that we have just attended the funeral of a rather eccentric friend who wanted to have her ashes scattered on the waters of a favorite pond. In this setting we have just noticed that the ashes of our friend have now been scattered on the surface of the pond. But think even further. We could then notice that as the ashes are scattered on the pond, the wind comes up and blows through a stand of ash trees. We have now stumbled on a scene illustrating the truth of "from ashes to ashes." Which statement about the different set of ashes is the truth of the scene?

One of the main criticisms of postmodern thought concerns the claim that the founders of modern thought, such as René Descartes, John Locke, Baruch Spinoza, and all the rest of the dead white European males, conceived the nature of the world as a limited set of clear, distinct, and self-evident truth claims. The postmodern critique is that these seventeenth-century philosophers assumed that there was one truth, one set of common assumptions, one set of sure foundations upon which all cognition must be based. One of the most persistent goals of modern thought, including the Enlightenment project, has been to find these firm foundations and to build our philosophies and society upon them. Kant further assumed that we could place religion securely and properly within the confines of enlightened reason.

No one doubts for a moment that the visionary quest of early modern philosophy was a magnificent endeavor. There were truly giants in those days, and we are all heirs to their common achievements. Nor should we forget that one of their motives was to try to find a way to overcome the devastating religious conflicts of the sixteenth and seventeenth centuries. If religious people could not settle their quarrels based on their shared Christian background, perhaps, so the philosophers reasoned, we could move to an even deeper level of common human sensibility and wisdom in order to escape from a constant state of religious wars. The philosophers' most enduring legacy, of course, was the development of the amazingly fertile matrix of modern experimental natural and social sciences, technology, and mathematics. The nagging postmodern doubt, in its more sober moments, pays a debt of gratitude to the work of these thinkers, but wonders if the assumption that there is just one set of foundational truths that can be ascertained by the human mind is really accurate or cognitively accessible to human reason. The founders of modern thought wanted to secure these foundations of all thought in order for humankind to build a new and better world, a shining city on the hill. The complaint is that we got New York.

The burden of the postmodern critique is that the early modern philosophers were misguided and overambitious in their search for unique and completely secure foundations for all knowledge. The moderns were not misguided in searching for truth, they were simply wrong in assuming that truth has one and only one sure foundation. In this regard, postmoderns are not so much "post" the early modern world of the seventeenth-century philosophers and the eighteenth-century Enlightenment public intellectuals but modernity's slightly dubious critics. Perhaps it is better to describe our world as late modern rather than postmodern. In a world of change and cultural relativism, it strikes the modern critic that we need to rethink some of the worldview assumptions of the Age of Reason.

Therefore, postmodern thinkers do not completely abandon the search for truth; rather, they redefine their goals and aspirations more modestly. Perhaps a metaphor will suggest the difference. To borrow from the great William James, postmodern thinkers believe that truth has a quality of emerging like drops of water; the drops are sudden in the sense that a moment before they were not there and suddenly now they are. When there are many drops collectively, these drops merit the name *rain*. They are creatures of their own contexts. The drops are surely wet when encountered without a hat or umbrella, but there is nothing like one universal water drop of rain to be found without its brother and sister droplets. They come as drops or not at all. Of course, we can apply common sense, logic, and advanced meteorology to thinking about the possibility of rain in order to be better prepared for it. James, least of all, would not want to push the metaphor too far. There are causal chains from the oceans to the atmospheric conditions giving us rain, not to mention the physics of liquids, that govern the emergence of raindrops.

Truth for postmodern thought becomes situational, contextual, transformative, and always relative to the perspective of the observer. It is just this set of features that bumps up against what many religious people believe is the truth of their faith—truth in the religious context is hardly relative, wiggly, indistinct, or vapid. Religious truth often flies in the face of any conventional wisdom, such as God's command to Abraham to sacrifice Isaac. It helps to note that this kind of postmodern critique is most devastating when deployed against a propositional view of truth, but less applicable to the truth of exhibition, action, or command as would have been the case if Abraham had sacrificed Isaac. But this still does not touch on another range of problems, especially when we see truth as a human quality of life and values. This human quality of truth demands a total commitment and, more often than not, gives rise to a sense of certitude that goes beyond merely saying that the faith is true as if it were a catalog of doctrines.

If we entertain the notion of truth being a quality of human life and character development, then we face another set of problems or opportunities. The human person is resolutely social. One of the chief characteristics of human life is that it embodies culture. In fact, from the time of the ancient Chinese sages, to take only one example from the collective wisdom of the Axial Age, it was noted that the learned discourses and the cultures they produced were one sure mark of the differentiation of human beings from the rest of the animate order. The great Confucian Hsün Tzu noted that many animals demonstrate intelligence, memory, and even isolated cases of virtuous conduct. Unlike Descartes in the early modern West, who thought dogs were just machines, Hsün Tzu was empirical enough in his observations to recognize that otters (or dogs if you like), for instance, were in many ways as intelligent and virtuous, or even more so, than some human beings. For Hsün Tzu, the next step in the animal world was the invention of culture. And culture depends on language to be passed on from generation to generation.

Language is a supreme cultural achievement. Without language there would be no human culture, because culture is not passed on genetically. Language must be learned anew with each passing generation. Without language we human beings would not be what we are, for we would have no culture. This means that we may be born as individuals, but we become persons in community. Parenthetically, this is the reason that the Confucian tradition places so much emphasis on the family as the first form of human community; I suspect that this is also why Christians embrace corporate worship, believing that the church is the pluralistic body of Christ. Confucius knew as well as anyone else that families were not perfect, but if society was to function at all, we need to pay careful attention to the family because it is in the family that we become persons with language and culture. It also appears to be the case that all religions have something to say about the importance of families as the locus of human virtue. Jesus also knew that gathered communities of worship were not perfect, as witnessed by the behavior of his own disciples and his criticism of the temple ceremonies of the day.

If human individuals as babies only become human persons through interaction with others in community, humanity is a social construction of reality. It is in this sense that we affirm and observe the relative nature of humanity. Our human social relativity here simply indicates the fact that we become persons in community, relative as related, and certainly not indifferent, to other people and to the divine reality. None of us is indifferent to our mothers, for good or ill, and few of us are indifferent when we grow older to the lure of divine things. No doubt something like this insight into the role of family and community resides at the basis of the notion of covenant as a central symbol of the Christian faith. A covenant is something even more basic than its specific stipulations, however interesting they may be. We are entranced by the beauty and symbolism of the rainbow God gave the world to make a crucial covenant with the world in the Genesis account, but this masks the even deeper fact that what is crucial for humanity is the connection with God and with each other. Covenants are plural if not symmetrical; the fundamental relationship to God is what is foundational for all the specific covenants.

Truth becomes an even more complicated matter when we realize the relative, relational nature of the human reality. The complexity is doubled again when we consider the following taxonomy. First, truth, and especially religious truth, relies on Buchler's threefold division of human discourse into propositional, exhibitive, and active modes. As we have seen, truth has often been identified as a set of clear, logical, self-evident, and foundational propositions. However, religious truth likewise encompasses the active and exhibitive elements of human life and hence is much harder to capture in a set of verbal propositions. We are grasped by religious truth and act accordingly. As it is said in the African American community, you have to talk the talk and walk the walk. Sometimes we even gracefully exhibit a truthful moment or action. Furthermore, postmodern theorists argue that the dream of a perfect set of truthful definitions of reality is a chimera of Enlightenment rhetoric. Clear and distinct lists of truthful statements defining reality may be a noble dream, and like a lot of rhetoric, point metaphorically toward what we know in our guts is true when we see or are grasped by truthfulness, but should never, like a good metaphor, be mistaken for the totality of events that make up human life. The great Taoist Chuang Tzu once likened propositional language to a finger pointing at the moon. True, Chuang Tzu said, it is useful for a friend to point out the direction of the moon for us, but once we have seen the moon, we do not need to keep on using the finger to find the moon. We can use our finger for other, different tasks.

Second, as if this whole set of issues were not complicated enough, just think what happens when we add more human beings to our landscape, people from other cultures, with other histories and other languages and customs. One of the fictions of the Enlightenment project was to define human beings as individuals, namely, beings essentially isolated from and unconnected to other human beings. But we now believe that this is too simplistic because we are persons only in community. It is true that we bear individual responsibilities and freedoms, but these only make sense within the fertile matrix of human sociality.

The story of the Tower of Babel illustrates the point nicely. God believed that human beings were becoming too potent because they were unified by a common language. In order to prevent human beings from becoming too powerful, God resorted to the simple yet profound stratagem of confounding the one human tongue into many mutually unintelligible human languages. While this may not rank with the expulsion from the Garden of Eden in terms of human tragedy, it certainly has been a curse and a blessing for untold generations as they struggle to learn other classical and modern languages.

We now live in diverse cultures defined by our separate languages and histories. All of our senses of propositional, active, and exhibitive truths are exponentially complicated and compounded by the vagaries of human linguistic specificity. After Babel, not only were languages confounded, human interaction became incomparably confused because we could no longer understand each other across cultural and linguistic divides. Is there any solution to this problem of human linguistic, cultural, and religious diversity?

The Buddha had a keen insight into the nature of this problem. When confronted with difficult questions, the Buddha argued that we must first distinguish between two types of conundrums. The first kind of problem may or may not actually have an empirical answer. The difficulty is that we may not yet have enough empirical data, and in fact, it may be almost impossible for us ever to gather enough data to solve the question at hand. For instance, just exactly how many fundamental physical particles are there in the entire cosmos as types and as a total aggregate? From what we know of the nature of the cosmos, it is difficult to see how we would ever be able to do more than estimate the scale of this question. Theoretically there might someday be an answer, but the chance of ever reaching the end of the empirical data appears bleak, especially when it may be the fact that new particles pop into and out of what we mere mortals call existence in milliseconds. The second kind of question is one that has no empirical answer. Many religious questions are of this kind. For instance, how could we finally decide if the universe is ultimately good, evil, or indifferent? Or, is the world eternal? Does it have a finite beginning and end?

The Buddha argued that when we find questions like this, it is not profitable for our spiritual life to dwell on them too much. They are like intellectual baubles, fascinating as far as they go, but not conducive to human insight and liberation. In fact, they are just the kinds of questions that sidetrack smart people from their proper goals. The example the Buddha used to illustrate the problem was a story about a person traveling in a forest. The traveler was suddenly struck by a poison arrow. A physician happened along and offered to remove the arrow and provide an antidote to the poison. But the traveler, obviously a philosopher, refused any succor until it could be ascertained who shot the arrow, what the arrow was made of, why the person wanted to harm the philosopher, what was the nature of the bow, the skill of the potential assassin, and on and on. The Buddha wisely pointed out that the wounded person would be dead long before even a few of the questions could be answered. Sometimes it is better to get on with life and not worry about the perfection of truth when truth is predicated on information that we will never successfully grasp. Or as I tell my graduate students as they struggle to finish their dissertations, the perfect manuscript is the enemy of the good, finished document. This argument, if not recognized by the eager and earnest students, is understood perfectly by their spouses.

In the modern pragmatic American tradition that began with C. S. Peirce and was continued by Whitehead, there is a suggestion about how to view the question of truth that fits well with our previous reflections. First, Peirce made the observation that we are constantly revising the truth. The reason for this is that, first, the world is always renewed and never static. This notion of constant renewal meshes nicely with the Christian claim that the world is constantly refreshed by the Holy Spirit. Second, Peirce, like the Buddha, believed that all of our truth claims are only hypothetical because they can never be perfected, either empirically or metaphysically. What we have are not clear, distinct, foundational theories of truth but rather corrigible hypotheses to be tested in the world as to their value and validity. We know them by their fruits.

As Whitehead wrote, the process of finding the truth is like an airplane ride. We begin on the ground of solid reason and accepted fact and then launch ourselves into the wild blue yonder. This flight allows us to look at things from a different perspective. From the new perspective we modify, if necessary, our previous assumptions. Then we return to the airport and test our modified hypotheses. Whitehead, like Peirce, believed that the process never ceases because the world is constantly renewing itself. Peirce and Whitehead are expressing one of the common features of the worldview of the modern world, namely, that the nature of nature is to change. This contravenes the much older ancient and medieval worldview that there are unchanging essences to the world.

In fact, according to Whitehead, the best that we can expect for our truth claims is what he calls an asymptotic approach to truth. Here Whitehead is quite like Calvin in one respect. Whitehead holds that the finite human mind, or in fact any created, finite mind, can never encompass the whole of the divine reality. This is Whitehead's homage to monotheism. If a finite human being could encompass all of reality, then there would be another being coequal to God, which is precisely what is denied by the definition of monotheism that there is only one God. Moreover, Islamic theologians argue, on the basis of the Qur'an, that the human proclivity to associate mundane and created things with the ultimate divine reality is a primal human sin and the basis for idolatry.

Modern Western people inhabit a vast cosmos of change and relationships, of powers and forces—this has become our paradigmatic worldview. This relational and processive worldview makes sense to us as we order our daily lives, even if it clashes with our previous theologies. Our task is not to bemoan the lack of conceptual fit. Our task is to preserve the ultimate goal of seeing, hearing, and doing the truth that will set us free. Having realized the social and changing nature of reality, we understand that pluralism is the natural condition of humanity. People wander across old religious boundaries because they seek, as St. Augustine said long ago, to rest truthful hearts securely and peacefully in the divine reality. Our task is the same as St. Augustine's search for God; we do Augustine no honor by merely parroting his historically finite theory of truth. Yet in all humility we must also understand that our understanding of truth will seem as quaint to future generations of humankind as the best of ancient astronomy and the theory that the earth was flat and the center of the cosmos.

CHAPTER 4

Baking the Bread of Marriage

While celebrating the thirtieth anniversary of the founding of the Boston Theological Institute, the local interdenominational consortium of nine regional theological schools, I was chatting pleasantly with a distinguished retired theologian about religious pluralism. While he had spent most of his career thinking about Christian social ethics, he agreed with the consensus at the dinner table that religious pluralism was a pressing matter for modern theology. Furthermore, he observed that our response to religious pluralism is fraught with ethical implications. For instance, if we demonize other religions, we are liable to treat persons as less than fully human, or as somehow inferior to us. Such teachings of contempt paved the way for the Holocaust and other genocides in Cambodia, Rwanda, and Bosnia. We all lament the destruction of the Native peoples of the Americas by war, disease, contempt, and neglect by the early European immigrants. One of the few bright points of the early Christian mission was the successful counterargument made by the Roman Catholic missionaries that Native peoples were fully human and should be treated accordingly. If only such treatment had turned out to be the case.

The dinner conversation then shifted to my report about another conversation with a group of over thirty theologians at a seminar in Boston. During the seminar I observed that interfaith and interracial marriages were much more common now than in previous generations. Just to make the point, I asked the seminar members how many of them were either married to someone from another religion or had a child who was married to a partner from some other faith. It astounded the group that all but two of those present fit the category of a family with mixed marriages. I even checked to make sure that this did not mean that a Methodist was married to a Catholic. It did not.

After I related this story to my fellow dinner guests, my distinguished colleague told me that he too had conducted a marriage ceremony for his son and new Jewish daughter-in-law. He told me that he had tried to be sensitive to the feelings of the young woman and her family; he spoke with obvious pride about this son's new family. The story illustrates a complex of issues, not all of them as pleasant as merely reminiscing about a wonderful family wedding. For instance, what are we to make of the fact that this was a marriage between a Christian and a Jew, a union considered with disfavor by the Jewish community?

From the Christian side there is nothing specifically more difficult about a Christian-Jewish marriage than any other interfaith union. But from the Jewish side, the pain of witnessing a growing number of such unions is very difficult, even disturbing. As is well known, the Jewish community does not allow for mixed marriages. However, although there are no firm statistics, estimates now suggest that perhaps 50 percent of Jews in North America are marrying outside of their faith. This is a matter of grave concern for the Jewish community. As far as I know, the Christian churches have never bothered to track the growing numbers of interfaith marriages. From the Christian side the crucial questions are, What do we make of the other religion? And what do we make of the fact that such marriages will almost automatically generate new forms of multiple religious participation?

Actually, interfaith marriages, rather like interracial marriages, are something of an embarrassment for most religious leaders. Such mixed marriages raise more questions than pastors and priests want to deal with. Therefore, mixed marriages are more likely to be ignored than celebrated; these marriages can also be rejected and the young family excluded from the religious life of both families. But the most common reaction is simply to ignore the special religious needs of the young couple and hope that the problem goes away. I have argued over and over again that this is a grave theological and pastoral mistake.

There are all kinds of reasons for the embarrassed neglect of interfaith marriages. First, it begins with the families themselves, who are often nervous about this kind of match. Second, the local minister also does not know what to do about these mixed marriages save for her or his own practice and experience in such matters. As far as I know, theological schools do not normally include instruction in officiating at mixed marriages. Of course, some denominations now do have formal guidelines for mixed marriages.

The fundamental theological reason for this lack of reflection is that the churches have not developed a theology of religious pluralism that allows them to deal effectively with interfaith marriage. At best, the churches that do have guidelines treat such marriages as exceptions to the rules. One of the reasons for this, especially among modern Protestants, is that they lack a coherent theological reflection on interreligious relations. Roman Catholics, of course, have recourse to the guidance of canon law in such matters. Nonetheless, Christian leaders approach, if they do at all, the question of religious pluralism as a truth function; namely, is it proper for a Christian to marry a Buddhist based on the formal teachings of the Church Universal? However, how in the world does a clergyperson meet a young couple in love and tell them that what confronts them is a confused set of truth functions? The notion of "truth" as a set of logical propositions is flawed when it comes to the question of marriage. What we have here is a proposal by the couple to establish a new family. The typical propositional view of theology is handicapped from the beginning in endeavoring to deal with an issue not built on propositional logic.

A perfect example of this kind of head-in-the-sand approach occurred while I was counseling with local Christian and Muslim leaders in a town in northern Ontario. A good Muslim friend, Professor

Mahmoud Ayoub, and I had been invited by a local Christian minister and the local Muslim community to talk to them about the upcoming wedding of a young Muslim man and a Christian woman. While the minister and the Muslim community leaders were obviously intrigued by the planning for the wedding, they clearly also had ambiguous feelings about it. They would go along with the wishes of the young couple to try to create a joint ceremony, but it was obvious that their hearts were torn.

Professor Ayoub sensed all the hesitation. He tried to draw them out, not just about the wedding itself, but what they were going to do for the couple in the future. Clearly this was not something to which either the minister or the Muslim leaders had given a great deal of thought. Professor Ayoub suggested that it was time that both parties gave it some thought. Ayoub and I both agreed that interfaith marriages are even more difficult than those between members of the same religious community. There are simply more pressures on the couple. With the divorce rate for new marriages rising all the time, with the pressures of modern life, the added difficulties of living between two religions is another burden for a young couple. It is even more of a burden when there is no support or understanding from either religious community. And then there is the question of children, since this young couple was looking forward to a new family.

The young couple themselves dismissed all of our questions; they were sure that their love would carry them over any hurdles life might place in their way. Ayoub and I were less sanguine. Again, Ayoub asked, What about the children? Would they be raised Muslim or Christian? The couple answered that they would worry about this later. The couple then had to leave for some other prewedding event, hand in hand and assured that the world would be as rosy as it now seemed in the warmth of a beautiful early Canadian fall. Again Ayoub and I were less confident.

Ayoub and I then asked the minister and the Muslim elders what they thought of this. Did they just want to wait and see what would happen? The conversation caused Ayoub and me to understand that although the minister and elders were happy enough to go through with this joint ceremony, they had not thought very much about continuing support for the couple. They were uneasy about what they could do for the couple. Professor Ayoub especially was not very happy to hear this news. He pointed out that unless the two communities were willing to support the young couple, then what really was going to happen was the creation of yet another alienated, secular young family. Professor Ayoub pointed out that this was going to be a very difficult time of adjustment for the couple, and if the Muslim and Christian communities failed to support them, then didn't the religious leaders realize that they were abandoning their pastoral responsibilities?

The rest of the visit went well for everyone concerned, but, on the flight back to Toronto Ayoub and I reflected on what we had learned. It saddened Ayoub that the community had put so much effort into inviting the two of us to visit and give advice, and yet was unwilling to formulate a concrete plan to support the young couple. We both agreed that the religious leaders were wonderful people who were actually making a great effort to do the right thing by inviting us to visit and by counseling the young couple as well as they could. The problem was systemic rather than personal. Ayoub noted that interfaith marriages were just something the communities would like to sweep under the rug. Or there was a tacit expectation that the couple would eventually decide to throw in their lot with one tradition or the other. However, the more likely outcome was that the couple would not go to either community because it would be more and more clear that the two communities really did not know what to think of them.

Interfaith marriages are difficult for the communities and for the couples involved. Again we must ask why this is the case. I will focus on at least three possible answers to this question. The first response is purely pragmatic. We are now witnessing a mixing of peoples caused by the expansion of travel and immigration unparalleled in human history. Actually, the massive transfer of peoples from Europe to the Americas began after contact in the fifteenth century but expanded dramatically in the eighteenth, nineteenth, and twentieth centuries.

While there were plenty of interfaith marriages, the mixing in North America was overwhelmingly between varieties of Christians, at least among the new settlers. The problematic area in the nineteenth and early twentieth centuries was marriage between Protestants and Catholics. These mixed Christian marriages were not met with any positive enthusiasm either.

What is different in North America at the end of the twentieth century is that people are immigrating in great numbers from Asia, Africa, and the Middle East. People of other faiths have always been coming from Africa, although they were forced to do so because of the slave trade. They theoretically were not allowed to marry the dominant white majority, although this obviously never stopped the mixing of the races. The contemporary wave of Asian immigration makes sense because many futurists argue that the twenty-first century will be the Pacific Rim century if not even more ecumenical in reach, including South Asia as well. Along with vastly increased immigration from South and East Asia, people from all parts of the world are also now arriving in North America. Just like previous waves of immigrants, they are bringing their religions with them.

There is a second factor we need to add to the equation. Due to the changes in immigration laws, the people now arriving in North America represent the best-educated cohort of immigrants the world has ever seen. Many of the new immigrants are professionals in education, business, law, technology, science, the arts, and medicine. If you don't believe this, make a short visit to any youth orchestra in any major North American city and observe the astounding talent and dedication of young Asian women to Western classical music. Or stop by any local medical school, science institute, or computer company.

Furthermore, these bright young people go to college in astounding numbers (the University of California, Berkeley, now has a freshman class more than half Asian and Asian American in composition). And we all know what happens in college. People fall in love and get married. The only deviation from the old norms of college life is that the young people meet a different ethnic and religious mix

than they did in the old days. Young people return home with potential spouses of all ethnic and religious groups. When I was growing
up in Oklahoma in the 1950s and 1960s, this was referred to in hushed
tones as the dreaded possibility of "miscegenation," or interethnic
marriage and children. Because of the present structure of North
American courtship patterns there is precious little parents can do as
an aggregate to stanch the flood of interfaith and interracial marriages. Young people of similar cultural and economic classes tend to
marry each other. In fact, the sight of interracial couples sometimes
no longer draws stares of amazement or reproach.

Third, while the question of love and marriage is daunting enough,
there is yet a second layer of the puzzle that needs to be addressed.
This is euphemistically called "the changing role of women" in the
modern world. It is often simply called feminism, but many women
who are part of the contemporary transformation of women's roles
reject the term *feminism* as implying a certain political spin for the
metamorphosis of their lives. Professor Ursula Franklin, the first
woman to hold the rank of University Professor at the University of
Toronto and a metallurgist of distinction, made the point to me and
a group of graduate students like this: it had been downhill for women
ever since the late Neolithic. This Stone Age collapse of the positive
roles of women as independent forces in society has just begun to be
reversed in the modern world after thousands of years of the exclu-
sion of women from political, economic, and social life.

Professor Franklin went on to say that it was difficult to say just
what these changing roles would ultimately mean for women and
men because the world since the Neolithic has had so little experience with powerful, liberated, and free women. Of course, Professor
Franklin noted, there have always been extraordinary women who
have carved out roles for themselves within a patriarchal world. Nonetheless, these women were the exceptions that proved the rule. Most
women were not free to play significant roles in the world beyond the
prime domestic unit, the family. Furthermore, it struck Professor
Franklin that no great cultural area had been much better than any
other. Neither Europe, the Islamic world, India, South Asia, East

Asia, nor the great civilizations of Africa or the preconquest Americas provided women anything like the rights and opportunities young women now take for granted. She stressed this point because she believed it was futile to make a "grass is greener" argument for one cultural area of the world—all classical, medieval, and early modern societies treated women in ways that outrage women today.

Anyone over fifty realizes how dramatic these changes have been and how irreversible they appear to be. With women now going into combat roles in the armed forces of the United States, there are no barriers to the accomplishments of women if they seek to master the requisite skills involved in a particular profession. I remember my father, an American historian, once telling me when I was young that a gentleman in the eighteenth century could follow the law, ministry, or the profession of arms. I suspect that it would not have occurred to him that women would fill these and other roles within his lifetime, though the changes have pleased him immensely. What changes will the inclusion of women in these traditional bastions of male performance hold for the future?

Alfred North Whitehead wrote that the domination of men over women was one of the last great barbarisms of the modern world. According to Whitehead, the subordination of women was a relic of the past, like slavery, and any civilized society ought to expunge the subordination of women from its midst. As we survey the modern world, it appears that the complete domination of men over women is fading, though not without a fight. Significant elements in all the great cultural areas of the world are struggling to put women back in their places. The cry is often couched in religious language. According to reactionary wisdom, one of the sure signs of the decline of any culture is when women run amok in a frenzied attempt to escape their traditional roles as obedient daughters, wives, and mothers. This discombobulation of gender roles indicates that women have the audacity to demand the same roles and rights as men on the basis of social and legal equality. The "amokness" of the changing roles of women is proved when women move beyond what had been sanctioned for thousands of years by the culture. The traditional roles for women were confined to children, kitchen, and church.

Fewer and fewer women are willing to listen to talk about re-
stricted social roles anymore. G. W. F. Hegel argued that once you
have told people that they are free, they begin to act as if they really
are free. This is precisely what is happening to many modern women
regardless of their age, social status, ethnic or religious origin, and so
on. These women will not go back into the cages of the past. They
demand the same freedoms that men have enjoyed for ages. And one
of the things that they require is the right to choose their own marriage partners. Of course, different women go about being free in
diverse ways. Some challenge male authority, some pretend to go
along with what men demand but subvert the actual outcomes, and
some just cheerfully ignore frustrated male chatter.

Surprisingly, the history of companionate marriage (i.e., marriage
that defines itself as a relationship of companions of equal worth)
originated at the opposite ends of the Eurasian landmass at roughly
the same time. Although the name *Puritan* conjures up someone
without a sense of humor or delight in sensual matters, it was just
these supposedly dour Puritans who invented the notion of
companionate marriage in the Western world. On the other side of
the world, a remarkable group of educated Confucian women in the
late Ming period (the end of the sixteenth and the beginning of the
seventeenth century) were arguing for companionship and education
as the sound basis for a real marriage. The Confucian women, on the
most impeccable scholarly grounds, argued that affectionate emo-
tion between spouses was a worthy goal for a marriage. Modern Chinese women are fond of quoting the old saying that women hold up
half the sky, but usually are still expected to cook, look after the children, and clean the house. Companionship did not and does not
always mean equality.

The pointed question that many modern women now ask is, How
do religions stand for or against the full liberation of women? Are
women to be allowed to play essential roles in their religious lives as
well as their personal and professional lives? This is a crucial question
because the church sometimes was one of the few places outside of

the home that women were allowed to play any kind of public role. While the traditional church roles for women were severely limited to service functions and auxiliary roles, at least they allowed women to leave their homes and to organize services for the community.

Moreover, women point out that one of the human institutions most in need of great renovation as regards the rights for women are its religions. Women register that religions, rather than offering liberation to women, have conspired with other elements of society in keeping women in bondage. Women see themselves as second-class citizens in their own churches. They are becoming less and less willing to accept these roles. Serving coffee and tea and mending the robes of the priests, monks, and pastors without any ability to set policy and take an active role in worship is less and less appealing to more and more women. Women are increasingly unimpressed with the argument that the domination of women by men has some kind of absolute social or religious warrant.

Some radical women theologians, such as Mary Daly, who has forsaken the Christian tradition completely, contend that there is really only one true religion in the world. It is patriarchy, the worship of male power. Although men pride themselves on their different religions, what all the post-Neolithic religions boil down to is the worship of a male authority figure (God or the gods). Furthermore, women were supposed to pay attention to and support special male social and religious institutions, with all their attendant paraphernalia of self-righteous male gratification and the denigration of nature and women. The second part of the patriarchal paradigm, the denigration of women, comes easy because women are linked to nature incarnate, as something beyond the immediate control of men. Women are the silly, sensual, flighty, and illogical part of nature. They are dangerous to men if they, like nature, are not under the domination and control of vigilant men. The paradigmatic women are Eve and Lilith, the source of the fall from the garden and the archetypal "bad" girl who knows her own mind and desires.

Mary Daly reasons that marriage is just another patriarchal ploy designed to keep women in bondage. That is why marriage is blessed, sustained, and refined by the various male religious institutions even when the priesthoods evince a distaste for women as concrete human beings. Daly's fervent appeal is that women remove themselves from both forms of oppression because there is little or no hope that they will be able to reform marriage or the church enough to be fit places for female habitation. Of course, other women disagree; some are relatively happy with their roles in society and others, while not pleased with all the features of their lives, believe that it is possible to rescue their religions from an oppressive past. Many modern women do not want to live without men, the historic religions, and marriage.

Moreover, these debates among and between women are almost always resolutely interfaith dialogues. The reason for this is that women share similar experiences with male colleagues in almost all religious communities. For instance, there has been a constant struggle over the past century for women to be ordained to the clergy in the Christian churches. This battle is now matched by similar movements in Judaism and Buddhism. The Buddhist women point out that they were allowed to be ordained much more frequently in the early days of the Buddhist movement than they are now. Like their Christian sisters, they want to return to a more egalitarian time, one more in tune with the spirit of the Buddha. Buddhist and Christian women point out that the Buddha and Jesus both shocked their more orthodox male religious counterparts because of their favorable treatment of and respect for women. But this is something of a digression from our discussion of interfaith marriages.

Furthermore, anthropologists note that cultures are most conservative about food customs and marriage. These fundamental social customs are some of the last that will be changed or given up without a struggle. They are even more persistent than language or dress. People are more likely to change languages than they are to change how they eat, or at least what their favorite foods happen to be. The same goes for marriage customs and choices. Therefore, any change in marriage patterns signals a fundamental change in the social life of a culture. In short, if you can convince a group of people to change their marriage patterns, you have effected a major change in their culture. And what could be a greater change than for a boy from Oklahoma to marry a Japanese Buddhist? Some might even argue that this is even worse (different?) than giving up a love of chili, beer, and football. Lilith, that forgotten first wife of Adam in the Jewish tradition, must be enjoying the spectacle of interfaith marriages from high heaven.

The rising number of interfaith marriages is astounding from an anthropological point of view; it is sometimes even more shocking to religious professionals. As far as I know, no major (or even minor) religious tradition has ever encouraged its members to marry outside the faith. About the only concession made was to accept the new partner as a convert into one or the other community of faith. I have heard many accounts of men and women who have endured classes about the other religion in order to marry the person they love. In some cases, these conversions based on love and marriage actually work because the new convert does indeed discover the divine reality in the faith of the new spouse and his or her family—sometimes.

What about when the couple wants to continue to take part in each other's religious life? Is it possible to be Jewish and Christian at the same time? Or Buddhist and Christian? Or Hindu and Christian? Or Christian and Confucian? Or Christian and Marxist? These are simple but amazingly difficult questions to answer. Let us dwell for a moment on how Hindus in North America are responding to mixed marriages.

I have chosen the Hindu community because it, like the Jewish community and many Native traditions, defines membership by birth. Traditionally, to be a Hindu was to be born of Hindu parents in India or other parts of South and Southeast Asia. But all of this is rapidly changing. London and Leicester in England are major Hindu cities. Toronto and Los Angeles are the same in North America. Pittsburgh has a wonderful Hindu temple. Moreover, children born of Hindu parents outside of India continue the practice of their religion in South Africa and Boston. But what about interfaith marriages?

Hinduism, like all other Asian religions, is a growing, flourishing addition to the North American religious scene. The emerging Hindu reality varies from recent immigrants from the subcontinent, to American converts and followers of various gurus, to immigrants from the Caribbean islands. The question of the relationship of these diaspora Hindu communities poses vexing problems for Hindu identity. In older days it was much easier to say who was and was not a Hindu. As we have noted, Hindus were born in India or South Asia of Hindu parents. Even to travel over the oceans to Europe or the Americas was tantamount to leaving the faith or being expelled from the Hindu community.

Hindu scholars are quick to point out that *Hinduism* is an English word that covers a vast range of experiences and groups in South Asia and beyond. For instance, there has never been anything like an organized, national, or international Hindu religious center or authority. Hinduism has always been a highly diverse reality, ranging from village custom to the most sophisticated philosophic and theological speculation of the learned elite. Some Hindus are devoted followers of one god; some worship many gods; and some schools of Hinduism even reject the notion of God altogether yet remain within the Hindu fold. The Hindu world stretches over many language families and has given birth to daughter religions such as Buddhism, Jainism, the Sikh movement, and many, many more diverse forms of divine worship and practice.

As far as community recognition went, the consensus was that to be a Hindu meant that you were born into the tradition. You were included in the Hindu tradition, which was often much broader than just its specific religious component. You were born into a broader society, sometimes even into a special economic profession. Although birth was crucial, a pious Hindu was expected to give credence to a special set of texts (the Vedas) and specialized interpretations of these sacred scriptures. It also generally meant that you followed a teacher of these Vedic texts associated with one of the major orthodox schools of interpretation and practice if you were a part of the educated male elite. You would live your life governed by the customs and the parallel traditions of the learned priests, monks, pundits, and duties of your caste and family.

Another major question that the tradition asked itself was, Can you be a Hindu if you are born outside of the subcontinent and the ancient Indian cultural enclaves in Southeast Asia? For quite a while most Hindus argued that to be a Hindu you must be born of a Hindu family in the subcontinent, or at least in the long-established Hindu settlements scattered throughout Southeast Asia and accept the Vedas as sacred texts. But by the end of the twentieth century it is less and less clear that this needs to be the case. The rise of the new Indian Diaspora is causing Hindus to rethink what it takes to be a Hindu. While birth in a Hindu family is still taken as a sound criterion for deciding if you are a true Hindu, the fact of being born in Pittsburgh no longer immediately disqualifies you from being a recognized member of the Hindu world.

Another vexing question has to do with whether or not you can join the Hindu world by conversion. While it is entirely possible, and even encouraged, to become a Christian, Buddhist, or Muslim, conversion is not always accepted by the majority Hindu community. For instance, there are intense debates as to whether or not the North American members of the Krishna Consciousness movement can be considered orthodox Hindus. The debate about this question continues undiminished. It is a pressing question for local Hindu councils. Whereas the Jewish community does allow conversion, the Hindu world has no such commonly accepted guidelines concerning what constitutes conversion to Hinduism. One of the methods Hindus have employed with Western converts is to call them Neo-Hindus, implying that their religion comes from Hindu teachings even if they are not actually recognized by the larger community as members.

Because of all of these questions, the desire of a young Hindu woman who is contemplating marrying a Christian is complicated on a number of levels. There is usually no question about her religious identity, nor is there for her husband. Hindus now have had centuries of sustained contact with the Christian movement in all its diverse forms. It is assumed that the fiancé will remain whatever he was to begin with. If this is the case with the father, what then will the children be in terms of religious identity? This is where it becomes perplexing. The second difficult question would be if the husband decided that he wanted to be considered a full participant in the religious life of the Hindu community. As is well known to sociologists, women tend to have a great deal to say about the religious tendencies of any family unit.

These are the kinds of questions that are being lived out in the daily lives of many couples in North America. Because there has never before been anything like this in the history of Hinduism (another effect of extensive immigration to North America), most of the solutions are ad hoc and governed by the wit, intelligence, and ingenuity of the local community. Actually, there has always been interfaith marriage in India as well, but nothing like the mixing that goes on in the open and pluralistic world of North America. Frankly, there have been interfaith marriages as long as people from different traditions meet each other and fall in love. The human skill at romantic bonding eludes even the most careful management of family and religious communities. Furthermore, Hindu colleagues understand that the question will be with them in increasing numbers as their children intermarry into the larger North American world. Intermarriage is a real test of the Hindu claim about how tolerant their tradition has always been toward others. It is also an experience that will ultimately enrich both the Hindu and Christian religious worlds.

The ingenuity of the Hindu community in adapting to its North American surroundings is helped because of their high educational background. The Indian immigrant community is the best-educated national aggregation ever allowed into North America, ensuring success in the professionalized world of modern North America. In many ways the persistence of the Hindu community mirrors its previous success and adaptability in Caribbean and African countries such as Trinidad and South Africa. A professor friend tells me, for instance, that she has a dream of teaching her University of Florida football team and student body how to chant "Go Gators" in Sanskrit, the sacred language of the Hindu Vedas. Centuries ago in India it was strictly forbidden for a woman to learn or hear the sacred Sanskrit language. But now it is her humorous aspiration to instruct the whole student body to chant "Go Gators" in Sanskrit as her contribution to victory on behalf of her university. As a North American mother of a fine group of bright children, she can also expect that they will go off to college and make their own marriage arrangements.

I have focused on the Hindu community because it is a paradigmatic example of a successful immigrant community facing the question of intermarriage; it is also a faith that does not share an extended history with Christianity in the modern world. Jews and Muslims, for instance, share a vast common history with Christians; there is always a sense of similarity when debating with them as dialogue partners. We are, as the Muslims say, the People of the Book and share a complex religious milieu. But Hindus were and are the prototype of the non-Christian for generations of North American Christians. If the Chinese were considered to be oddly nonreligious, Hindus were thought to have strange gods and many of them. On the one hand, Hindus, like most Asians, have been serenely uninterested in the Christian invitation to convert on any massive scale. But on the other hand, Hindus have been fascinated by the Christian message and the person of Jesus. Mahatma Gandhi, the liberator of the subcontinent, read the New Testament with pleasure and for spiritual guidance. Once asked about Western (read Christian) civilization, Gandhi said that he thought it would be a wonderful idea. Furthermore, Martin Luther King, Jr., revered Gandhi as a spiritual teacher and traveled to India as a pilgrim intent on learning from the saga of India's nonviolent struggle for liberation. The circle was completed between East and West, between Gandhi and King in their quest for freedom and social justice.

Hindus even have a time-tested method of dealing with other religions. They simply incorporate what they like into the Hindu pantheon. For instance, Jesus, like the Buddha before him, is well on the way to becoming an incarnation or avatar of the Hindu divine reality. I have seen devout Hindus seriously explain to Christians that they are already Christians because they have accepted Jesus as their personal savior. They pray to Jesus and chant his sacred name. However, they do so within their own understanding of religion. They point out that Jesus remained a Jew to the end of his life, so why should they be asked to convert to a new community of faith if the master did not? Sometimes Christian missionary work has truly unanticipated results. What are Christians to make of the Lord Jesus as a Hindu avatar?

A more intense form of the debate rages around the question of Jewish-Christian intermarriage. To begin at the beginning, it is always necessary to remember that Christianity began its life as a Jewish sectarian outreach to the gentile Greco-Roman world. It was, as my rabbi friends remind me, Judaism for export. The greatest proponent of the mission to the gentiles, of course, was St. Paul. Although the peripatetic saint was pleased with his new churches, one wonders if even he would have been astounded by how successful his mission to the gentiles became. The Christian mission, after it became gentile in nature, never had any marked success within the Jewish community. As the final transformation from Jewish sect to Christian church occurred at the end of the Greco-Roman world, a number of fierce debates and firefights arose on both sides of the rapidly growing fence between synagogue and church.

It is fair to say that the great West Asian religions, Judaism, Christianity, and Islam, have cut their teeth on exclusivistic teachings, doctrines that argue that you cannot be a member of more than one religious community at a time. While the Jewish community was reconstructing itself after its defeats and humiliations at the hands of the conquering Roman Empire in the first and second centuries of the Common Era, the emerging Jewish community in exile from the Jerusalem temple differentiated itself from other quasi-Jewish groups. One of these was the Christian church, and whatever else the early rabbis thought about Christian forms of doctrine, faith, and practice, they were definitely of the conviction that the church was no longer a recognizable part of the Jewish family. In fact, if you became a Christian you could not remain a Jew. On the Christian side the same kinds of exclusionary choices were also made. To be a Christian meant that you could no longer be a practicing Jew.

These mutual antipathies obviously extended to intermarriage. Although Christians allowed marriage to non-Christians in the Greco-Roman world, this was only done with the fond hope that the spouse would convert to the one true faith. On the Jewish side, and this extends into the modern period, when someone marries outside the faith, Orthodox families mourn the convert as if he or she died. The long and short of these and other arguments are that Jews and Christians developed a highly refined sense of who was in and who was outside their orthodox traditions. The Islamic community, although adding its own idiosyncratic spin to the debate within the family of the People of the Book (the Islamic term for themselves, Jews, and Christians), inherited this keen nose for exclusionary thought and practice.

This exclusive sense of finely trimmed hedges between religious communities is so common now for the People of the Book that most Jews, Christians, and Muslims take it for granted. It is merely part of the religious air that we breathe. Moreover, because Judaism became a minority movement in both the Christian and then the Islamic worlds, the strictures against interfaith marriages were as much a way to preserve the community as to protect the unique nature of the Jewish religious heritage. To question such rigid separation between religions, and what could be more challenging than interfaith marriage, seems to fly in the face of the way God wants the world to work. In fact, as we have already seen, there are even hallowed pejorative theological terms for these kinds of questions and acts. The most famous labels are syncretism, idolatry, and apostasy. But somehow I doubt that full-blown religious and theological syncretism is in the mind of couples contemplating an interfaith marriage.

This is a good place to remember that there are other voices to be heard. In East Asia, for instance, interfaith marriage is thought much less strange. In fact, it hardly seems strange at all. Buddhists, Confucians, Taoists, and Shintoists have been marrying each other for thousands of years without the destruction of any of their communities of faith. The wonderfully precise sense of sharp religious boundaries manifested by the People of the Book has always struck East Asians as peculiar to the West Asian religious scene. Many East Asians not only marry from other communities of faith, they also believe that they can practice certain parts of the other tradition without seriously distorting their own fundamental beliefs.

Western intellectuals (and this includes Muslims as well) find this cheerful mingling of people and religion disconcerting. It so bothered some early Roman Catholic missionaries that they concluded that they would have to teach the Chinese elementary Aristotelian logic even before they could preach the Christian gospel. The Jesuits argued that anyone promiscuously mixing religions could not think logically, and because Christianity was logically the only religion of salvation, you needed to understand logic in order to understand true religion. As we now know (partially because of the brilliant intercultural interpretations of these missionaries), the Chinese understood logic perfectly well. In East Asia there were even thinkers, some Chinese, Korean, and Japanese Neo-Confucians and Buddhists like Nichiren, for instance, who agreed in part with their learned Jesuit confreres about the benefits of keeping religions separate and pure.

One of my favorite Neo-Confucians, Ch'en Ch'un (1159–1223), spent a great deal of time arguing that Buddhists and Taoists were mistaken about reality in general and human relations in particular. Buddhists and Taoists were too otherworldly for Ch'en's taste as a realistic and pragmatic Confucian scholar. However, it never would have occurred to Ch'en to forbid marriage between Buddhists, Taoist, and Confucians. For instance, Buddhism appealed to a great many Chinese women, and there are numerous records of devout Confucian sons memorializing the Buddhist piety of their beloved mothers and grandmothers. What the Neo-Confucians did was to give more and more of their daughters a sound Confucian education in the hope that the true teachings of the sages would keep them away from Buddhist or Taoist irregularities and excesses. Nonetheless, there were many dedicated Confucians who grew to love and respect Buddhism and Taoism from the examples of their wives and mothers.

None of this pleasant urbanity prevails, however, in the Western world. One of the ironies from the Jewish point of view is that the political situation has changed so dramatically over the past twenty centuries. At the beginning of the split between the Jewish and Christian worlds, Judaism was the robust parent and Christianity was the struggling child. Nothing is more intense than a family rivalry, and it sadly sometimes degenerates into terrible hostility. Over the centuries the Christian churches turned on their mother. They said and did cruel things to her. As Rabbi Jordan Pearlson of Toronto once said to me (I think that I remember the statement accurately), "Two thousand years of Christian love would make anyone nervous."

From the Jewish perspective, interfaith marriage is a serious issue. First, it is considered wrong according to Jewish law and tradition. Second, and this is extremely important for Christians to understand, it is considered a threat to the very survival of the Jewish community. Many Jews see interfaith marriage as yet one more assault on their community by the gentile world. Interfaith marriage is insidious because it arrives with the face of hopeful love without prejudice or anger. The marriage is proposed because the non-Jew loves the Jewish spouse-to-be. Nonetheless, from the Jewish perspective, this continues to mean that the world loses another Jewish person.

Because of these and other mixed (mostly negative) feelings, almost no Jewish religious leaders will counsel or officiate at interfaith marriages. Although liberal Christian clergy will officiate, after the ceremony there is usually little special support for the new couple. However, members of mixed marriages recently have taken the situation into their own hands. They founded a magazine called *Dovetail. Dovetail*'s reason to exist is to support Jewish-Christian families that are serious about their multiple religious commitments.

The founders of *Dovetail*, after realizing that they could expect little support from either community, decided to practice self-help. They began with a newsletter, which grew into a magazine. The magazine now reaches tens of thousands of subscribers. It offers solid advice about how to secure an interfaith marriage. I confess that when I was first told about the project a few years ago I never anticipated its stunning success. I did suspect that there was a real need for such material, but I failed to realize how eager people were to take the profound question of interfaith marriage so seriously.

Dovetail now not only publishes its journal but has also branched out to commission other education resources. There is even a wonderful little book for children about how to visit their Jewish and Christian grandmothers. All of the material that the editors produce is not, let me repeat, designed to create some new kind of religion. It is not syncretism. Quite the contrary. What strikes anyone reading *Dovetail* is its commitment to a mixed religious life. The editors inform their readers how difficult this will be. Neither community of faith will really accept what they are trying to do for themselves and for their children. Yet the fact that tens of thousands of couples are willing and eager to teach respect for both faiths is inspiring.

One of the things that the *Dovetail* people are doing is to transform the Christian teachings of contempt for living Judaism into respect. They know from their own lives that difference does not mean inferiority or superiority; it simply means difference. They are not trying to replace one tradition with another. These couples are trying to cherish each other's religious commitments and to pass this knowledge down to their children.

If there ever was a profound undertaking of multiple religious participation, it is surely enshrined in the work of *Dovetail*. Another point also needs to be noted. The leadership for this project has been provided by women. The original idea was generated by women. If these women, committed to interfaith marriages, could not get any solid support from their religious institutions, they decided to create their own support network. They provide information about what works and what does not work in sustaining their marriages and in educating their children. They tell others about what to expect as they move along in the natural life cycle of a marriage. They are participating in at least two religious worlds. Their fervent hope is that they will be able to be faithful to both their Jewish and Christian realities. Only time will tell the level of their success. But at least they now know that they are not alone and that they can ask others for support and information. They are creating a whole new set of rituals, relationships, experiences, and wondrous recognition of a mutuality in marriage that mirrors divine love for the creation of new life.

It is a commonplace in the study of religion that men think they run the show. But it is the women who support the edifice with their care and finances. Women do not often become reformers in the classical male model of someone who directly challenges the church establishment. They simply do something different, so different that it changes reality. This image of the passive female religious life is changing as women move into positions of leadership in their communities of faith. When women begin to tell their daughters that it is OK to enter into an interfaith marriage, no one is going to turn the clock back to a religious world with strict boundaries. The walls between and among faiths are being erased, combined in modern companionate marriages around the world.

CHAPTER 5

The Soufflé of Meditation

A diversified spirituality business is booming in North America. Wherever you turn there is a teacher, therapist, or guru eager to offer her or his distinctive modern rendition of classic spiritual meditations, contemplations, postures, prayers, chants, and practices. Nowhere, save perhaps in an interfaith marriage, is there more experimentation with multiple religious practices and nowhere do people wander farther from their natal religious than when they are in search of a new form of meditation or contemplative prayer. In fact, the term *spirituality* is becoming so popular that it threatens to replace the older term *religion* altogether in some people's understanding of their faith practice.

Moreover, nowhere is the search for new forms of spiritual cultivation more intense than in college, and beyond as people seek goals for their lives. In college, students are exposed to new ideas and new religions. Suddenly the churches that they grew up with are no longer the only opportunity to express their desire to explore divine things. Moreover, we live in a culture that encourages young people to think for themselves, to experiment with life. Is it any wonder that some of them will hanker after new wisdom and forms of meditation? After college, when they are beginning their careers and families, it becomes clear to them that they really do not have to return to their natal religions, especially when these local churches cannot provide what they are seeking.

One of the things that intrigues college students is meditation. Of course, not all of them develop any form of practice, but they have learned about it and have begun to wander around and wonder about the wider world of religious pluralism. New forms of meditation allow young people to pursue their spiritual quests without becoming committed to any one religious institution. People in their twenties and early thirties are notorious for not joining religious institutions. It is usually only when they begin to have children that they search for a religious home.

One of the engaging demographic facts of North American religious life is that Buddhism is the most rapidly growing religion in the region in terms of percentages if not absolute numbers. After I announce this finding to my classes of potential Christian ministers and pastors, I tell them not to be too shocked or worried immediately about having to think about serving a Buddhist congregation. I point out that the Buddhist community is very, very small in absolute numbers. However, it is growing and having an impact on North American life every day. All we have to do is think about the various film actors and actresses who are involved in supporting the Dalai Lama. Some, like Richard Gere, are sincere followers of Tibetan Buddhism. Television characters with Buddhist names like Dharma would have been inconceivable even twenty years ago.

When I am asked by the curious about the rapid growth of Buddhism I usually have two answers, depending on my mood. The first is that Buddhism is simply a fascinating and worthy religion all by itself. Having studied and taught Buddhism at the college and graduate level for twenty years, I have no difficulty understanding why people fall in love with the profound teaching of the Buddha's *dharma*. My friend Professor Lee Yearley, who teaches religious studies at Stanford University, calls this my personal case of spiritual regret. This means that I love Buddhism as an appreciative outsider. I have taught the tradition in a way that students sometimes ask me if I am a Buddhist. I take this as a compliment because it means that I at least approximate the sound of Buddhism. I tell my students that I am not a Buddhist and privately pray that I have done no harm to the *dharma* by my academic instruction. But I have never had the slightest inclination, despite my profound love and fascination with the Buddhist world, to ever take refuge, as the Buddhists say, in the Buddha, *dharma*, and *sangha* (the community of Buddhists). From a Buddhist point of view I am a supporter of Buddhism but not a member.

Yearley argues that we need to develop new virtues to go with the new times, including ways to deal with religious pluralism. Working within the grand tradition of Western virtue-based ethics of Aristotle and St. Thomas Aquinas, Yearley maintains that virtues need to be expanded and even new ones invented when we face novel situations. Of course, classic virtues such as justice and courage remain because human beings find themselves in situations in any culture and time when they must be brave and just. It is impossible to conceive of a human society that would not need just and courageous women and men. We now live in a time of intense religious pluralism. Yearley thinks that we can deal with this situation by developing a new virtue to fit the situation or try to adapt older virtues to meet the needs of the time. For instance, another term for the reaffirmation of a classic virtue is what Spinoza called *fortitudo* or "strength of mind." According to Spinoza, *fortitudo* allows us to be in touch truthfully with the beauty and truth of the world and to conduct ourselves in a poised way in terms of the strength of resolve tempered by the true and the good.

In the case of religious pluralism, we can apply the virtue of toleration for minority opinions and beliefs. However, Yearley argues that we need to do better in the present period. As more and more people learn more about other religions, and in fact make room in their lives for other forms of practice, meditation, and piety, we have moved beyond mere toleration. We need a new virtue to guide conduct. Yearley calls this the virtue of spiritual regret. The virtue of spiritual regret helps us to appreciate another religion and assists us in realizing that we cannot, as much as we love the other tradition, become a member of it in any full or complete sense unless we formally convert to it. Even though we have grown to understand another religion, it is not our ultimate spiritual home. We may enrich our own religion with new insights and practices, but we remain resolutely within our own community of faith. Spiritual regret moves us beyond toleration into the new world of mixed religious practices. Like all virtues, it needs to be refined, and there is no perfect way to describe the golden mean spiritual regret seeks because each human religious life is unique.

The second answer about the rise of Buddhism has to do with the growing North American interest in meditation as a spiritual discipline. Buddhism is only one of the many new ways North Americans are reviving the arts of meditation. While it is true that all religions have forms of meditation and spiritual practice, no one has been better at presenting these ancient forms of spiritual discipline than the Buddhists. From the chanting of Pure Land Buddhists to the silent sitting of Zen practitioners, when many people think of meditation, their images are formed by contact with Buddhism. Pragmatically the various Buddhist teachers have provided classical and tested forms of meditation reformatted for a lay audience. This has happened because Buddhism has come to a new world in North America and has had to learn how to present its wisdom and spiritual disciplines afresh to an audience that knows nothing of centuries of Buddhist theory and practice.

Meditation and spirituality are slippery words to define. Like the concept of religion itself, they can be stretched to cover a vast range of practices. Here again the idea of a metaphor or prototype is helpful. Our image of meditation is probably that of a person sitting in a lotus position, hands on the lap, eyes gently focused a few feet ahead, in profound silence. We recognize someone practicing meditation from this metaphorical prototype. Like pornography, we know it when we see it, even if the Supreme Court always finds it devilishly difficult to define in precise, propositional terms. However, what is important to note is that practice is key for meditation. Of course, there are theories about meditation, but they are not as important as practice. In this regard, meditation is like ritual; it is something that you do for its own delight. Later it may be profitable to think about what you have done, but the crucial thing is always the practice.

Moreover, the practice points to a specific picture or image of what meditation is as we noted above. George Lakoff and Mark Johnson argue that one of the primal foundations of knowledge and thought is the human reliance on metaphors. Lakoff and Johnson memorably call these "the metaphors that we live by." It is easy to make fun of metaphors because they often become clichés. Nonetheless, conventional wisdom is still wisdom. The argument for metaphors goes like this. When we think of a bird, most speakers of English will think of a robin as the prototypical image of a bird. When we see other creatures we think of as birds we compare them to our robin; this works well with most birds, but we sometimes will have to stretch the metaphor of bird when we encounter owls or penguins.

The beauty of Lakoff and Johnson's method is that it gets us around the thorny problem of deciding on a perfect propositional definition of meditation because when we see it, just as when we see a bird that looks like a robin, we know we have found someone in meditation. One of the features of the Western intellectual tradition going back to Socrates, Plato, and Aristotle was the rejection of the use of metaphors and examples as the preferred way to define true knowledge. What these founder figures wanted was a strict definition that did more than just point us in the right direction. However, when we think of Jesus' teachings we can see how powerful a metaphor or parable is in teaching about religious matters. Let the wise go and figure; I believe that Jesus would have approved of Lakoff and Johnson's reminder that the world is made up of metaphors to live by and not just strict propositional definitions of reality. Reality is metaphorical and only then propositional, though propositions and logic have their profound value as guides to clear thinking about the application of metaphors.

Let me enter another caveat. I do not want to suggest that there is anything wrong with seeking a clear definition of meditation or anything else for that matter. It has become fashionable to decry the Western Faustian drive to get clear about words and things. Linked to this rejection of logic as a guide to life is a rejection of reason as well. To reject conceptual and propositional clarity as an aid to clear thinking is just as muddleheaded as to maintain that such intellectual clarity is the root of all thought without recourse to other dimensions of human life. I remember a casual graduate student friend at the University of Chicago who was working in the more refined reaches of philosophic logic and decision theory. He was studying with a professor renowned for working on the strict and rigorous formal logic of decision making.

My friend was in love, and his lady was pressing him to consider marriage as a serious option. This was really more than just an option, as even the most potentially absentminded male professor in the making knows; it was a demand for some kind of decision and commitment on my friend's part for a domestic future. Then it struck him that his academic research was in the field of the application of logic to decision making. He cheerfully reduced all of his thoughts and emotions to the proper mathematical equations and proudly showed his work to his teacher. He wanted to make sure that he had the right formal equations and that he had not made any silly mistakes in reaching his conclusion.

My friend went off to see his professor and we agreed to meet in the coffee house of the Divinity School later that morning. I was there first and saw my friend arriving with what can only be described as a bemused expression. I immediately asked him how it went. Well, my friend said, his professor patiently listened to his explanation, and then blanched. The first thing the professor said was, "My God, this is about real life, not logic!" He then went on to share whatever human insight he had about relationships. At the end the professor returned to the equations and told my friend that he had done a good job but that he should not be governed by those results; this was a place for the poetry of the soul, according to the professor. The professor ended their meeting by pointing out that this was a decision that needed the best reasonable thought and a careful examination of my friend's true feelings.

If we are shown a picture of a monk or nun sitting in what looks like quiet contemplation, we will call this meditation. This is our present prototype for meditation, and it is not a bad one really. This is our meditational robin, our bird of the soul. The use of metaphorical thinking persuades us that it is unlikely that we will ever stumble upon a perfected definition of all the various modalities of what the religions call meditation. Besides, I believe that people today are inventing new forms of meditation that will break the molds of previous forms of spiritual discipline. For instance, laywomen are now practicing meditation and they will surely develop new patterns that suit their needs as daughters, friends, lovers, spouses, mothers, and grandmothers—and busy professional women as well. They will not be like a male robin, but they will still set the birds of their souls in flight toward the divine reality.

In Toronto we experimented for a number of years with joint Buddhist-Christian meditation. To begin we invited respected meditation teachers from both traditions, in this case, from the Anglican and Tibetan communities, to design and carry out the joint project. There was a wonderfully amusing moment when the two meditation teachers became very firm with the other two organizers, myself and a fellow Buddhist university professor. With compassion and humor the meditation teachers pointed out that as professors we loved to talk about meditation. In fact, we had drawn up a preliminary plan that called for as much talk as meditation, and of course, we began with learned disquisition on the history of meditation in both our traditions. On the contrary, the meditation teachers said that they would prefer to have us meditate, based on only the most basic preliminary instructions, for at least three-quarters of the weekend seminar. Only after the practice could we talk.

The meditation teachers pointed out that only after meditation would we have something to talk about. They were in favor of talking, but only about the actual experience of sitting, chanting, praying, or walking. Our practice was to devote alternating weekend sessions, with up to fifty participants, to Christian and Buddhist meditation. Our spiritual exercises included quiet sitting, some meditative walking, and silent prayer. Our two teachers told us that they were using basic beginning techniques common to all meditative traditions designed to still and focus the chatter of our minds. One of our common metaphors, drawn from the rich imagery of the Chinese world, was of learning to recognize the "monkey of the mind." The Chinese say that our minds are like fun-loving monkeys. They race about from thing to thing and never concentrate for long on anything. Here again the teachers told us that they could lecture on the structure of their tradition, but the real goal of meditation was its practice. The proximate goal was to calm the mind; the ultimate goal was to allow the person to be in touch with the divine reality or their own Buddha nature.

For practical purposes, I will only offer a functional definition of meditation. Meditation is what experienced, competent, and spiritually gifted meditation teachers teach. Each teacher and each tradition will have a different take on what they offer to their students. For instance, one of the things that both of our Buddhist and Christian teachers reported was that what they were doing had been first perfected for the monastic communities and orders of which they were part. However, these hallowed practices could, with some modification, be taught to laypeople as well. Both teachers were emphatic that this was a good idea and as far as they were concerned, these wonderful practices had for too long been locked behind the walls of the monasteries, temples, and convents. What works for monks and nuns also works for laypeople. They laughed when they told us that the meditations might even be more beneficial for laypeople because lay life was so much more complicated and conflicted than the quiet routines of monastic life.

Another term is inextricably linked to the popular modern use of meditation. This is spirituality. If ever there was a slippery, protean word in the general vocabulary of religious people, spirituality is now it. To those who favor spirituality, it means everything opposite to the deadening rigidities of all other forms of modern religious life. If you are on the other side of the debate, spirituality simply means a mindless fascination with any religious fad that happens to wander down the pike from bioenergetics to yoga, deep ecology, and goddess worship. *Fuzzy* hardly begins to describe all the ways people define spirituality.

I find spirituality used more by young people to indicate their perceived differences in religious preferences from their parents. But it is certainly more than just a typical intergenerational tiff. I take spirituality to define a broader spectrum of beliefs and practices than meditation. It bespeaks an alternative worldview. Perhaps most crucially, beyond whatever specific meaning we attach to spirituality, it speaks to a deep longing in the human spirit that we become connected to the source of our life, however we define it. This connection can be to the living God of Jews, Christians, and Muslims, to the divine, formless Godhead, to high Hindu theology, or to simply understanding the way things really are in Theravada Buddhism and many forms of Chinese Taoist and Confucian reflections on the Tao.

The origins of this passion for a new spirituality lie deep in the religious history of the Western soul. One profound reading of this need comes from the work of the German sociologist and historian of religion Max Weber. Weber, in contradistinction to other social scientists of his day, took religion seriously. He believed that we could only understand the social world if we understood the religious history of humankind. To this end Weber provided us with a brilliant reading of the relationship of modern Protestant religion and its secular culture. In order to explain the relationship of religion and culture, Weber posited the notion of "inner worldly asceticism" to describe a characteristic form of early modern Protestant spirituality. In short, having rejected Roman Catholic models of spirituality as too clerical in nature after the Reformation, the early modern Protestant thinkers made work in the world a form of religious piety, a form of spiritual probity. Working as a merchant capitalist was transformed from being spiritually suspect into being spiritually transforming. If you need a metaphorical prototype, think of Ben Franklin and all his witty sayings about the virtue of hard work.

According to Weber, the early Protestants were successful in linking hard work as a religious calling in the secular world to the engine of their spirituality. They developed science, technology, and most of all, the powerful intellectual tool of technical rationality to govern all aspects of their lives. The Catholic Counter-Reformation, and especially the Jesuits, carried out much the same task for Roman Catholics. What all these diverse reformers did not foresee is that technical rationality would take on a life of its own. What started as dedicated service to the Lord by means of diligent labor became in Weber's memorable image an iron cage for the spirit. The whole panoply of economic skills that were designed to liberate people instead became their masters. What started out as a quest to build that new and shining city on the hill ended with the local mall and rampant consumerism, a veritable ecological and spiritual cancer. Weber wryly noted that every great success brings in its train a host of unanticipated consequences.

The modern spirituality movement, like its parent Romantic reaction of the nineteenth century to the dark, satanic mills of the early industrial revolution, is trying to liberate us from the iron cage of our own success in terms of secular modernization. We gained the world and lost our souls. When people talk about spirituality we should listen carefully because it is here that we can sense the eternal drive of the human soul for something better, something liberating, something true, something divine. When my students tell me with complete candor that they love their Protestant heritage and are excited about what they learn about Chinese Taoism, I do not laugh at all. They are right from my point of view because they are searching for the workings of the Holy Spirit.

The key term here is lay audience. Again, I want to stress that all religions have forms of meditation, usually as sophisticated as the Buddhist teachings, but they do not, at least in North America, teach them to laypeople. It is the laypeople who are now hungering for meditation in great numbers. I need to make a more careful distinction, however, between the Protestant denominations and Roman Catholic and Orthodox churches. For instance, although she would never have used such strange language to describe what she did, my grandmother prayed in front of the beautiful altars of her parish church with her rosary constantly moving in her hand. This was her form of meditation, and an effective one at that. I know that her granddaughter (no longer part of the Christian movement) does none of these things. Even if the granddaughter were a Roman Catholic, one doubts that she would spend much time with a rosary at the local church. The piety of my grandmother's pre–Vatican II world seems distant. But my sense of distance from her piety and meditation practices says a great deal more about me than it does about my grandmother.

The point of my family history is that there were effective forms of prayer and meditation available to laypeople in the past. But what about the Protestant churches? Definitions matter at this point. On the one hand, if by meditation you mean something as complicated and focused as even the most simple forms of Buddhist meditation as taught by any number of competent Buddhist teachers, then there is nothing like that in modern North American Protestant life. On the other hand, if you define meditation as a prayer life and the more ecstatic forms of congregational worship, then Protestants also have forms of meditation. Here again the African American churches provide a clear example. Anyone who has had the pleasure of worshiping with a Black church knows the power of prayer, the power of the rhythms of the preacher rising to the summit of the sermon while being constantly encouraged by the shouts of the congregation, or the power of the choir to raise the congregation to new heights of fervor.

I am much less sure that we can stretch the definition of meditation to include the Anglo congregations I inhabit. I remember once returning from a week at the Hampton Institute, that grand and historical annual June gathering of African American pastors, preachers, and musicians. Hampton is a stirring week of workshops on preaching and music, focusing on all the best worship styles within the Black churches. It is powerful and never dull. I immediately traveled to a nameless ecumenical meeting of a large professional theological society. As is the case with many such meetings, we began with a prayer service. I literally went to sleep; it was so boring that the only meditation I was able to sustain was to try to keep from snoring. Maybe the Spirit was there for other people, but it was not for me. I would have preferred to have been transported back to the Hampton Institute or a Buddhist-Christian retreat in order to contemplate the state of my soul.

There are some signs that this spiritual drought is beginning to change in the Protestant world. Congregations are hungry for spirituality, and what they often mean by this is some form of meditation. Often the minister is the last to know about this hunger. True, she will sense a yearning for spiritual nurture on the part of her flock, but most of her congregants will not be able or willing to tell her what they want. Some will be afraid to tell her that they find their need for meditation met by the local yoga or Buddhist insight meditation teacher. Some of the young women and men will even be training with a karate master who includes meditation as part of the martial arts training in order to show how a calm mind is as effective, or more so, than perfect biceps. I often find that the pastor is astounded to discover that many of her parishioners are doing this sort of thing. As in so many other areas of church life, the minister is the last to know interesting things about the congregation. Having been taught that they should not stray from the one true path, the members believe that the minister will be shocked or saddened to learn that they are taking spiritual sustenance somewhere else.

The real problem here is, even if the pastor wanted to teach meditation, could she? Most modern pastors would probably be too busy trying to fix the leaking roof or balky boiler; they are visiting the sick, working on endless committees, counseling, and preparing sermons. But even if a pastor had the time or inclination, would she have had the training? My experience as a theological educator tells me no. She might have had a course or two on prayer, but that would have been about the extent of her training in anything resembling the meditative arts. However, there is a growing movement in Protestant seminaries and schools of theology to add courses in spirituality that go beyond the occasional course on corporate or personal prayer. It is now recognized that unless the pastor has a solid spiritual foundation for ministry, the chances of burnout increase dramatically. Eventually you must calm yourself enough to ask, What does it all mean, Lord?

Furthermore, select seminaries are constructing specialized courses of instruction at various graduate levels for persons committed to a ministry of the spiritual arts. Along with the classical discipline of spiritual direction, simple forms of meditation are high on the list of skills necessary for such a ministry. It is precisely at this point that a great deal of interfaith work takes place. Christian students find that they are welcomed in many Buddhist and Hindu meditation centers. Some are even exploring roads not taken in the Christian past such as the traditions of the Celtic church. It is in these settings that they find the skills necessary to teach basic forms of meditation. Women venture even farther afield, seeking connection with the ancient traditions of the goddess and the feminine spirit of Wisdom.

There is something poignant in the fact that most often it is Protestant seminarians who must turn to other traditions for any effective spiritual training. They seek guidance from Roman Catholic and Orthodox teachers, Hindu gurus, Buddhists monks and nuns, and Native American elders. Actually, this merely replicates the religious history of humanity. As I have noted before, human religious history is a story of constant borrowing and modification. No religious idea is so securely bolted down that it cannot be appropriated for uses beyond the wildest dreams of its founders.

Worship in African American churches testifies to the creative nature of the divine deli. African Americans were torn from their African homes and religions and forced into slavery in the Americas. At first their new white masters did not want to share Christianity with them in case the slaves got the point about the liberation of the Hebrew people from bondage in Egypt. However, over time, most African Americans became Christians. But as scholars of African American religion have shown, there are ancient African roots in their patterns of worship and piety that differentiate their churches from Anglo churches down to today. The music, the patterns of sermonic call and response, the sense of organic community recall habits of the heart that even the whip of slavery could not drive from their souls.

I am constantly humbled by the fact that the African American churches, less involved in formal interfaith dialogue than the white churches, have such a rich interfaith heritage. I often get the feeling that because of this heritage, African American theologians wonder what all the fuss is about when it comes to religious pluralism. African Americans, as W. E. B. Du Bois wrote about at the beginning of the twentieth century, were an interfaith and intercultural people from the very beginning because they had no choice in the matter. As a minority people they persevere with a pellucid awareness of the complex task of living in different cultural worlds. For instance, the local imams from the Muslim community are included in various African American clerical alliances; it would never occur to these Christian pastors to exclude their Muslim brothers and sisters. Furthermore, African American theologians are right to remind the white churches that they must examine their consciences concerning interfaith realities in order to distinguish between genuine theological concerns and mere persistent racism.

As we have mentioned before, one of the perplexing features of meditation is the question of religious neutrality. Many teachers involved in teaching meditation have talked to me (and others) about whether or not some meditations are merely neutral techniques for calming the mind or whether the forms of meditation always contain the seeds of a specific religious tradition within them. The question here is actually a real theological issue. Are there any neutral religious forms? Very aware of this potential problem, Cardinal Ratzinger's office has issued a warning to Roman Catholics about the potential dangers of misusing meditational techniques borrowed from other religions. The cardinal believes that this borrowing may not be as innocent as it seems. It could be more like a Trojan horse introduced into the heart of Christianity.

The strongest argument against borrowing from other traditions is the claim that any religious form bears organically within it the seeds of its natal tradition. Hence, a Buddhist form will always carry a Buddhist message. If a Christian takes up a Buddhist practice, this will make the Christian something of a Buddhist, even if he or she does not know this to be the case. I wonder again about my grandmother and her rosary. Would it have bothered her to learn that was an ancient Buddhist practice transmitted to her via the Muslim world?

I hazard the guess that my grandmother would have smiled, or perhaps even frowned, at another strange interfaith factoid delivered by her ever-eager grandson. She probably would have ignored it, as grandmothers often do when confronted by the novel ideas of their grandchildren. She probably would have put in a good word to the Blessed Virgin Mary on my behalf; young men are prone to come up with such strange ideas even if they mean well in their youthful enthusiasms! But what about more recent borrowings, such as the heavy traffic in meditation techniques moving around our small world? When do borrowed ideas cease being novel and become simply another part of the religious food for the faithful?

This is a worthy question. In some cases, people do not even want others to borrow from them. For instance, Native American elders often talk about "wannabes," people, who after the most minimal acquaintance with Native spirituality, claim to be able to perform traditional ceremonies. Nowadays there is a great deal of debate within Native American religious communities about how much of their heritage can and ought to be shared with non-Native peoples; there is universal distaste for non-Natives recklessly making use of Native patrimony. I've had Native colleagues tell me that this is just another form of imperialism. First the non-Native people conquered the land, then they rounded up the Native peoples and tried to destroy their languages, cultures, and religions. Second, irony of ironies, they have changed course and tell Native people that they want to steal their ceremonies. No thank you. Although some Native elders are now pleased to share, and some are not, their ceremonies and teachings, they do so by instructing non-Native peoples about the non-portable nature of their religious beliefs.

Native religious teachings, which often involve profound meditations, fasts, vision quests, dancing, and chants, are perfect case studies of when religious practices can be moved from one religion to another (and when not). Many times Native elders have told me that their ceremonies are place specific; they are linked to the land given to their nation and lack meaning outside of that site. Nor is it place specific in the sense that certain Christian rituals can only be performed in or at consecrated sites, such as an altar, chapel, or cemetery. The elders teach that there is an indissoluble bond between the specific ritual and a given place, the place of the ancestors. My Chinese friends understand this sense of place as well. They will go to great lengths, for instance, to make sure that their parents and grandparents are buried in the traditional family home. Anything less would be unfilial in the extreme. My Chinese friends will even carry out a temporary burial until the time when they can transfer the remains of their elders to the proper burial place. My Native elders tell me that you cannot move a ritual from its place; it then simply has no meaning, is useless, or even defamed.

Of course, there are other Native ceremonies that are highly portable. In fact, I have heard the Sacred Pipe and its various ceremonies called a portable altar. My dearly remembered mentor, Art Solomon, told me the tale of his travels to the island of Mauritius in the Indian Ocean with his Sacred Pipe to take part in a planning event for the World Council of Churches' Sixth Assembly in Vancouver, 1983. The only thing that really worried Art about the adventure was that the Sacred Pipe should only be handled by him in a reverent fashion and he was worried, with good warrant, about having to go through French Customs in Paris on the way to Mauritius. Art could speak some French, but not enough, he feared, to be able to explain how the Sacred Pipe must be treated. In a perfect case of interfaith cooperation, Rabbi Jordan Pearlson from Toronto was on the same interfaith planning committee, representing the Jewish community. Rabbi Pearlson speaks excellent French and was able to carry out the negotiations with the French Customs agents. Art Solomon and Jordan Pearlson later told me that the French were wonderfully understanding of their needs and were both courteous and fascinated at the same time. Once at the planning meeting, Art used the Sacred Pipe to bless the work of the group; on other occasions, he could be scathing about the misuse of Native religious traditions.

This brings us back again to a perennial tension in religions between the universal and the particular. Religions affirm that their teachings are true and hence universal in the way that all true, good, and beautiful things are universal in scope. But some things are specific to each tradition. Until there was such an increase in interfaith cooperation and multiple religious participation, few religious people had to worry about the origins of their practices. Even if, as was the case for the rosary, the practice had come from outside the original orbit of the community, the massive gravity of tradition had safely locked the rosary into its proper place in the solar system of faith.

Let us return for a moment to the beach in South Carolina where the university chaplain used a Theravada Buddhist form of mediation, known as insight meditation, to work with her Christian flock. She told me that she did it for at least two reasons. First, she was convinced that her students needed to calm their minds in order to hear the small, still, quiet voice of the Holy Spirit. She went on to argue that we live in such overstimulated times that it is hard for anyone to listen for the guidance of the Holy Spirit. We all need ways to focus the mind in order to receive the blessings of the Spirit. But why, you ask, use a Buddhist form of meditation? The reason was simple. Many of these students were reacting against the congregations out of which they came—as one young woman told the chaplain, she would do anything as long as it did not remind her of her mother. Anyone who works with college students knows both their desire to spread their own spiritual wings and their desire to separate themselves from what they perceive as the hypocrisy or irrelevance of adult religious institutions. Yet here they were on the beach, practicing insight meditation.

Second, the chaplain used insight meditation because it worked; she told me that she had been taught nothing like it in her seminary education. She was not hostile about this, but merely reflected with me that teaching meditation was not a strength in Protestant theological education. Like so many other people, lay and clergy, she had come to insight meditation driven by a need to open herself to the divine reality.

The key point the chaplain made was that insight meditation was one of the universal, portable practices that works as well for Buddhists as it does for Christians. She hypothesized that this was the case because this basic form of meditation made use of the foundations of human mindfulness. It worked because we are all human and share the same basic brain structures. As a South American Native elder once told me, painkillers for dental surgery work for him and for other people all the same. The elder, like the chaplain, also believed that some forms of meditation functioned much the same way; they calm the mind so that a person could be aware of something beyond the flutter of daily events and stresses, joys, passions, delusions, and anger.

This is the universal aspect of religious life. We are all human beings with basic biological, emotional, and cultural needs. However, each culture defines and refines these needs differently. I love the next story told to me by a Native American elder because I suffer from a Confucian-Christian, that is to say, Calvinist-Methodist plus Neo-Confucian, compulsion to be punctual. Max Weber said that one of the characteristics of the Protestant worldview was a love of efficiency. Of course, in order to be truly efficient, everyone must be on time. No culture in the world has placed more emphasis on the measurement of time and punctuality.

The story began innocently when my friend told me about a visit he made to the Navaho Nation in Arizona. After he had been talking for a while, an older elder approached him and posed the following question. Looking at my friend's wristwatch the elder asked, "What does it do?" My friend said that it told time. The elder looked somewhat skeptical. My friend immediately went on to say that it would tell him when it was evening. The elder started to show real concern and asked my friend whether or not he would notice the sun setting without the little thing on his wrist. "Well, if you put it like that, of course I would notice the sun setting," my friend continued. Trying again, my friend said that the watch also told him when to go to lunch. By this time the Navaho elder was truly concerned. Would my friend really not be hungry without the little thing on his wrist? At this point, a revelation hit my friend and he said, "No actually, all this watch does is have the little hands go round and round." The elder smiled and said that was what he had always really thought watches did. The moral of the story is that different cultures deal with the rush of time in different ways. My friend confided that his Navaho elder thought it odd to say that time was in a rush. Only a culture that believes that time flies is going to design ever more complicated watches.

Some simple forms of meditation are like watches; what we do with them depends on other cultural factors. However, when we begin to put content into our meditations, then the ground shifts. For instance, it does matter whether we contemplate the Blessed Virgin Mary as the mother of God or dwell on the boundless compassion of Kuan-yin. We are not just stilling our minds, getting rid of the flotsam and jetsam of daily life, when we are reminded of Mary's infinite love and Kuan-yin's boundless compassion. When we think of Mary and Kuan-yin, we are beginning to form our life around the narratives and metaphors of the great religions of Christianity and Buddhism. In some cases the differences between the forms and content of meditation seem trivial, but then, sometimes they are not.

If you are a young Asian American you have inherited, along with a modern North American worldview and lifestyle, the classical traditions of Asia. Among other religious forms, this heritage, depending on whether you are an East or South Asian, includes Buddhism, Hinduism, Islam, Jainism, Sikhism, Taoism, Shamanism, Shintoism, and Confucianism. What do these traditions teach about emotional responses to the events of the world? For instance, neither Buddhism nor Confucianism teaches that we should just react to the world in any unreflective fashion. Rather, both teach that we must learn to look deeply into our fundamental being and react appropriately and ethically to the situation at hand. However, the Confucians believe that we must perfect all the range of our emotions whereas Buddhists are inclined to say that we need to guard against and eliminate anger, lust, envy, and so forth. Why do the Confucians disagree? Confucius once noted that if you repaid everyone with love and kindness, what would you have left for cases when you witness true evil in the world? As the centuries have rolled on, Confucians have cultivated the image of the wise teacher, the good friend, the prudent minister of state, and sometimes even martyrs to truth in the face of intolerable moral dilemmas. Although Asian traditions may appear alike to the untutored Western eye, there are subtle differences in their social ethics.

Nonetheless, Confucius himself, the very image of the sage if ever there was one, was a nobleman of virtue in an aristocratic world. He had strong opinions about right and wrong. One must resist evil, and it is entirely appropriate to feel righteous indignation when confronted with true human perversity. While Confucius certainly would have understood the Buddhist ethic of universal compassion and the Christian vision of turning the other cheek, he was a warrior of virtue who, when confronted with undeniable evil, fought against it with blazing anger. What makes Confucius a sage is that he would release the anger in a timely fashion. One of Confucius's many titles was that of the timely sage. This does not mean that he was punctual for his meetings. It means that he cultivated the proper emotional response to any situation, whether good, evil, or even humorous. In the medieval period, Christians became chivalrous knights and Japanese warriors became Zen Buddhist samurai.

Of course, these various distinctions between universal, neutral, and religiously particular forms of meditation mean little when we realize we live in an age when the heretofore sacrosanct boundaries of religious identity have become porous. I firmly believe that Buddhist teachers of meditation are now enriching the Christian tradition just as Greco-Roman intellectuals helped to fashion early Christian theology as the church moved from being a Jewish sectarian movement to being transformed into a daughter religion suffused with a Greek philosophic theology. I have already mentioned the introduction of the rosary as a means of meditative piety and prayer. In the realm of the mind and scholarly tradition, we need only reflect on the vast contribution of Muslim philosophic theology to St. Thomas Aquinas's grand Christian synthesis. Although we do not often think of it that way, the works of Aquinas are wonderful representations of multiple religious participation.

I do not believe that Aquinas would have been quite as nervous about the borrowing of meditation techniques from other religions as Cardinal Ratzinger appears to be today. Aquinas always believed that he was writing about the whole science of theology, and not just the Christian tradition. In fact, the notion of Christian theology as somehow separate from the cosmos, as my great teacher W. C. Smith once noted, would have struck Aquinas as impious. The divine reality is one, and whatever truth there is in the world, created naturally or revealed, is God's truth regardless of the religious label finite human beings put on it. The Muslims wisely say that reason is God's finger on earth; Aquinas agreed that we need to read the divine text accurately. Buddhist meditation for laypeople, especially laywomen, will enrich the Christian world as surely as reading the original texts of Aristotle as transmitted by the Muslim world opened St. Thomas Aquinas's eyes to new vistas of divine love and order.

CHAPTER 6

The Environmental Stew

It has become more and more clear that we are in the midst of a grave ecological crisis. Few would dispute the fact that the human community has fouled its nest. If the scientific community is to be believed, we must now even question whether or not human beings are a viable species. I will not bother to chronicle the growing list of problems that range from the destruction of the ozone layer high above our heads to the constant degradation of the water table below our feet. In the middle zones of common habitation, entire species are dying all the time; fish, amphibians, plants, and other animals are departing forever into the oblivion of extinction.

Though some diehards pooh-pooh the mounting empirical evidence, I would challenge anyone to visit the world's major cities and say that the environment is in good condition. Of course, this would mean visiting at a time when the smog was not so bad that you could see the ugliness of our urban landscapes. And if an urban outing is not enough, just visit what used to be "nature" outside of the cities to see what is happening to us as a species. Unfortunately, not only are human beings poisoning each other, our industrial infrastructure is also killing off other species at an amazing rate.

The late Carl Sagan spoke to an international interreligious conference in Oxford, England, in 1987 about religion and ecology. Sagan began by reminding himself and the audience that twenty years before he never would have been caught dead addressing a religious meeting. He believed firmly that science had replaced religion as the true source of human wisdom. The problems of the world were amenable to scientific inquiry and technological rectification. However, the intervening decades and the escalating ecological crisis caused Sagan to change his mind about the role of religion in the modern world.

Sagan believed fundamentally that the ecological crisis was one of values. The problems were caused by how people chose to live their lives: how many cars they bought, how much meat they ate, how much electrical power they used, and how many new gadgets they had to have. The power of consumerism and individualism, greed, envy, and even the just desire for a sustainable life in the developing world were all questions about the kinds of values human beings live by. These questions, Sagan thought, were ultimately moral. They were and are questions about our lifestyles and our impact through our economic and technological actions on the environment. When moral questions are asked not about proximate ends, such as returning a lost wallet full of money to its proper owner rather than taking the money, but about the ultimate aims and goals of human life, then morality moves into the realm of religion. Moreover, religions have always considered ethical reflection as part of their responsibility for humanity and creation.

The ecological crisis reveals yet another major fissure in the diverse patterns of Christian social thought between conservatives and liberals. The debate is about the personal, individual nature of morality or its collective, corporate nature. In short, if we seek the good, do we start with ourselves and our families or do we also pay attention to the large social world? Liberals, while never denying the need for personal rectitude, argue that many moral problems have a social component that cannot be addressed on an individual level. On the other hand, conservatives, using the banner of "family values," argue that the social engineering of the Great Society reforms of the 1960s ultimately failed because they sought to replace individual rectification with social handouts.

In terms of the fierce arguments in the contemporary world about human rights, the same debate is played out on an international scale. Western defenders of "human rights" affirm that there are fundamental rights that accrue to individuals and not collectives. For instance, I have the right to freedom of conscience, speech, and religious belief, not in the abstract, but as the specific person that I am. However, many thoughtful people in the Jewish, Christian, Islamic, Hindu, Buddhist, Native, and Confucian traditions would add communal, social rights to the list of personal rights and freedoms enshrined in the United Nations' Universal Declaration of Human Rights. They want to see communal and economic rights given the same legal standing as purely individual rights such as private property rights and freedom of speech, assembly, and conscience.

There is a great deal of truth on both sides of the debate. In fact, most people are willing to grant the legitimacy of both individual and communal rights. For instance, Americans prize the freedom of organizing their health systems without recourse to the European and Canadian patterns of a unified national health system regulated by the provincial and national governments. On the other hand, Americans also demand that the state and federal governments regulate and protect them from their own HMOs. In short, Americans want both individual freedoms and governmental (i.e., communal) protection.

What about the question of the environment? If ever there were a clear example of the need for social, communal ethics, this is it. One person, or even a whole religious community, is powerless to turn things around. Of course, this does not absolve us from doing what we can locally. We can and must strive to lead a more frugal, sensible lifestyle; we can support local recycling and more fuel-efficient autos, but none of these personal actions will have the global reach necessary to save the ozone layer from further thinning or some small fish in the Colorado River from extinction. Environmental ethics are communal ethics. This is why conservative religious leaders are often part of the network of people who reject the idea of an ecological crisis. Of course, conservatives agree that we must do better in conserving nature and natural resources, but their powerful distrust of collective ethical choices makes it hard for them to join the ecological movement because of its collective and holistic nature.

Furthermore, Sagan argued that religions, among their other functions, are the repositories of ultimate human moral values, both personal and collective. While he did not want to reduce religion to morality, Sagan deemed it impossible to think of ultimate moral issues without becoming religious. Here he was following the teaching of the great Protestant theologian Paul Tillich, who defined religion as the focus of our ultimate concerns. Sagan said, "Show me your ultimate concerns and I will show you your real religious convictions." On a more mundane level, we can expand this epigram into "Show me what you desire, what you consume, and I will show you your actual religion—regardless of your professed religious commitments." For institutions such as the church and business corporations, show us your "bottom line," show us your budget and we will show you where your real values lie.

Sagan reached the further conclusion that the ecological crisis was so all-encompassing that its solution demanded the attention of all humanity. As he pointed out, not even a frontal attack on the crisis by the two great superpowers (at that time the Soviet Union still existed as the other great superpower) could do anything about the problem until and unless every nation and all people agreed to do something about the crisis in a truly global fashion. The only people who were in any position not to point fingers at the others were the few intact Native cultures. Sagan directly summoned the collected representatives of the world's religions to do something about the issue before it was too late. Sagan's prayer was that it was not too late for us to reverse the downward spiral of damage caused by the effects of modernization over the past two centuries.

Of course, the roots of the ecological crisis are complex. There is no single cause and no single solution. Sagan was correct that it is such a universal problem that it demands universal cooperation. There is no single Christian answer, no Buddhist, no Muslim, no Jewish, no Jain, no Hindu, no Shinto, no Sikh, no Confucian, no Taoist, and even no Native solution. All of us consumed, drove, ate, and enjoyed ourselves into the mess, and we will have to find collective ways back out. But beyond the complexity of the issue, it is crystal clear that one major problem is that there are so many people living today (roughly six billion) compared to any time in the past. And if that were not enough, all of these people are consuming prodigious amounts of renewable and nonrenewable resources at an accelerating rate each and every day.

Nor, to be completely candid, does the sense of urgency about the environment pervade all religions equally, as we noted in our brief discussion of the difference in worldviews between conservative and liberal religionists. There are two sources of doubt about the real nature of the status of nature and the ecological crisis these days. The first has to do with religious perspective. Recently, odd as it initially sounded to me, a Taoist priest suggested that the environmental crisis was just another Christian version of the end of time. The priest asked to be allowed to be somewhat skeptical about the nature of the crisis. With not just a little bit of ironic humor, he pointed out, very politely, that crisis thinking was so typical of Christian theologians that he asked us to consider for a moment if we were not importing into or projecting onto nature one of our favorite Christian pastimes. Christians love a crisis. Furthermore, the New Testament concludes with Revelation, an apocalyptic vision of the end of the evil mundane world, followed by the cosmic, perfect renewal of creation. With only one lifetime for a person to make the decision for Christ, so the Taoist figured, all times are times of crisis for a Christian.

After I got over the shock of realizing that my fine Taoist colleague actually doubted that we were in the middle of a vast and dangerous environmental crisis, I had to pause for a moment. Taoism as a philosophic and religious tradition has a proud and profound ecological heritage. Taoists have always protected the sacred groves, ponds, marshes, streams, and mountains of China. I remember reading over and over again the exasperated comments of my favorite Neo-Confucian philosopher, Chu Hsi (1130–1200), who noted that whenever he went out into nature, he invariably found that the most beautiful and naturally vibrant locations were already the sites of Taoist monasteries (if Buddhists hadn't gotten there first). Even in the Chinese setting, one of the main functions of the Taoist tradition has been to calm the worried and frenetic Confucian conscience. One of the key teachings of Taoism is *wu-wei* on "uncontrived action." The modern Taoist priest wanted to do the same conceptual trick for the agitated Christian soul as well. But was the priest really right about the present state of nature?

The second point of controversy comes in two parts. First, one of the most difficult attitudes to overcome, even when, unlike the Taoist priest, someone recognizes the extent of the crisis, is the serene faith in the salvific abilities of modern science and technology. For instance, many people are now willing to agree that there is a problem with the environment. However, they are sure that once the questions of saving the environment are taken in hand, there will be modern scientific means to address the issue and to avert the impending disaster. They link this faith in science to the hope that improved technology will also mean that we will not have to change any of our preferred lifestyles. Of course, they are correct in stating the obvious conclusion that we will not be able to reverse the damage to the environment without the aid of science and technology. An industrialized world has no choice in this matter. As a case in point, they draw attention to new air-conditioning technologies that are not, at least for the present, deemed to damage the environment. They take this to be a perfect example of the fact that we will not need to adjust our lifestyles or suffer much personal discomfort if we really apply the full power of science to the ecological problems at hand.

The technologically secure optimist argues that modern science and technology give us abilities to shape nature undreamed of in previous eras. Yes, the ecological opposition agrees, but they are more concerned with human pride and the iron law of unanticipated consequences. They counter that although science and technology are powerful tools, their application always and everywhere creates unanticipated results. At the turn of the century it was calculated that the great cities of North America and Europe would soon be buried under piles of manure generated by the horses needed to transport provisions to the rapidly growing urban areas. But in the nick of time the perfection of the internal combustion engine and the invention of the automobile saved us from drowning in horse poop. It was about this time too that heroin was touted as a cure for morphine addiction. The moral that ecologists draw from these and other examples is that untested cures can turn out to be worse than the disease if we are not careful.

Or who would have thought that we would be living in a digital age immediately after the scientists at Bell Labs invented the transistor? Moreover, the Chinese government now has the technology, will, capacity, and ability to build the tallest buildings in the world in Shanghai plus the greatest dam in the world in the majestic Three Gorges of the Yangtze River. But what will the outcome be for the people of China once the huge Yangtze has been dammed? The optimist notes that the river will then provide an immense and ecologically sound source of renewable energy for the Chinese people. Other colleagues counter by saying that the whole thing will silt up in a couple of decades unless huge amounts of this new energy are directed back to the constant dredging of the gigantic lake formed behind the dam. So the debate rages. Yet it seems that our collective modern faith in science and technology remains unbroken in either the East or the West.

The second objection to the beneficent power of science and technology moves in a completely different direction. This objection encompasses a whole range of what are called eco-justice concerns, one of which is anger in minority, poor, and inner-city communities that they have become the dumping grounds for all the toxic wastes unwanted in the more affluent parts of the globe. Poor people and people of color have noticed that the new technologies of the environmental cleanup industries, which are often quite toxic in and of themselves, are located in their neighborhoods and not in the wealthy suburbs. Internationally, many poor countries in Africa are seduced into becoming the new dumps for the waste of North America and Europe. All of these concerns focus on questions of social justice. Is it fair for the poor of the earth to have to pay an inordinate price for the ecological salvation of the wealthy?

The issue is further complicated by the fact that many countries in the developing world wonder whether or not this is not just another ploy on the part of their former colonial masters to keep them in a form of modern servitude. What they now hear is that the governments of the rich and powerful Northern world have realized the errors of their ways and strongly urge the developing South not to follow in their footsteps. Unfortunately, it is precisely these steps of modern technology and industrial development that made the North rich in the first place. Sorry, the North says, but you, the South, will not be encouraged to develop in the same way the North has done. To many Southern ears this means that they are being effectively denied the opportunity for any kind of economic development at all. Their only role is to be the toxic dump for the world and for new environmentally safe mineral, agricultural, and forestry companies controlled by the Northern corporations, including industrial East Asia.

Many analysts from the Third World see this as a recipe for continued underdevelopment and poverty. They go on to note that the Northern world is unlikely to practice any kind of distributive justice in the immediate future. The Republican Party's Contract with America in the mid-1990s was not predicated on increasing international aid for the impoverished of the world. Some have even argued that, following the slang of the Mafia, it was a contract *on* the environment itself. The new neoconservatives love neither the American poor nor the international poor; they also cast scorn on international agencies that suggest that the United States should mend its prodigal and wasteful economic ways.

In facing these kinds of complex issues, ecologists frame the immense scale of the ecological dilemma as a drama in three major parts: consumption, development, and population. From a religious point of view, what is the root cause of the problem? The first thing to notice is that all of these roots of the crisis are inextricably linked. Environmental scientists describe the combined effect of the three as the impact or footprint of humanity upon the natural world. But is the present problem or range of problems unique in human history? Definitely yes. With the phenomenal growth in human population during the past two centuries there are more people alive today than in the whole previous history of the world. We are probably all aware of the population projections for the next century. They are not encouraging. In fact, in some parts of the world the population pressure has become so grave that governments have been forced to act decisively. China, for instance, has a drastic policy of one child per family. It is only in this way that the Chinese believe that they will be able to stem the growth of their population into the third millennium.

At present the American religious right has reacted with indignation to the Chinese population policies. But what else are the Chinese realistically expected to do? If the religious right has something better to suggest than an immediate conversion to Christianity and market capitalism as the only way forward, the Chinese would be delighted to hear it. Needless to say, the Chinese government and people are not impressed with the logic of the dual conversion proffered them in the name of God and mammon. I have made the population problem as stark as I can because I believe it points to a real area where religious doctrine and practice bump up against the ecological crisis. Although the scientific community has not reached any conclusive answers, it does appear that there may be too many people in too many places for the earth to sustain.

But that is just *the* problem, isn't it? Those secular humanists devoted to fundamental human rights and the religious right both intensely dislike the Chinese approach on fundamental but separate grounds. The whole issue of population is so fraught with potential interreligious conflict that many environmentalists shy away from directly confronting it. Or if they deal with the population question at all, they try to effect change incrementally by indirect methods. For instance, advocates of women's rights and environmentalists have observed that one sure way to stanch the population explosion is to increase the education and well-being of women around the world. Education and a personal sense of worth have proved to be the most effective contraceptives ever discovered.

Of course, the only sure way the well-being and education of women can be provided for in the developing Third World is through development. This desire for development generally means accepting Western modernization and secularism at the same time. This returns us to the complexity of the problem. It seems that a solution to one part of the equation means the addition of yet more freight in another tormented part of the body of Mother Nature. Conservative Roman Catholics and Muslims agree that there is a religious command to increase the human race. However, no sane member of either of these religions wants the birth of myriads of babies followed by their immediate death through starvation. Like all human beings, they hope for human flourishing. The question, as always, is how.

According to many religious traditions, the root of the problem really lies in the desire for more and more consumption. In fact, the Buddhist tradition teaches that the main reason we find ourselves in this predicament in the first place is our insatiable desire to grasp those things we think make us happy. Hsün Tzu, one of the great founders of the Confucian tradition in the third century B.C.E., pithily defined the problem like this: human desires are infinite, natural resources are finite. From the Confucian viewpoint, environmental problems were to be solved through learning how to curb inordinate consumerist desires and by careful governmental conservation policies. All in all, Hsün Tzu's analysis was not a bad prescription for solving some of our problems. Many Christians can remember a time when greed and envy were considered faults and even sins.

In terms of our three root problems, consumption as a form of grasping greed (to coin a Buddhist-Christian term for the all-too-human failing) is the most susceptible to a religious consensus as far as a possible solution goes. No religion, large or small, has much good to say about the unbridled desire for simply lusting after more and more material things. More insight into God or the divine reality, more charity, more kindness, more virtue—that is another matter entirely. However, the received wisdom of the religious community is that desire, when uncultivated and unrestrained, only leads to problems too numerous to catalog. Of course, religions such as Judaism, Islam, and Confucianism, just to mention three prominent examples, have teachings about the proper enjoyment of wealth and things of the world justly and proportionately obtained. Not all sober religious thought demands that we renounce the pleasures of the world. The real trick is not to be dominated by our desires for things beyond reason and morality.

The problem for the modern world is to decide whether we will follow the path of religious cultivation as disciplined, rational, sober, and moral action or consumer society as a form of moral cancer, with growth and the mantra of "more and more" as its only goal. Consumer society, as embodied in late industrial market capitalism, reigns supreme in the world today. The global reach of the multinational corporations, the chief instruments of consumer society, defies even the best efforts of regulation by the most powerful nation-states. The threat is not subtle. If you do not play by our rules, the multinational corporations will then move their capital and plants out of your country entirely. It is ironic to note that this does not mean that the corporation head and his or her family leave the comfortable and safe confines of New York, Paris, Bonn, London, or Tokyo for India, South America, South Asia, or Africa.

With the fall of the communist societies of Eastern Europe and Asia, what alternative is there? A. N. Whitehead suggested that true metaphysical principles, that is to say, principles that guide the entire world, never take a holiday. That is why they are so hard to find: we can never notice them because of their absence. Modern corporate capitalism now resembles Whitehead's first principles: it never takes a holiday. With the advent of the electronic digital world, the capital flows around the world without pause. When markets close in New York they will be awake in Delhi, Singapore, Hong Kong, Shanghai, Seoul, London, Paris, Berlin, and Tokyo. There is no place that these markets cannot reach.

The market as a modern economic system shares a common feature with the modern scientific and technological mind-set we previously outlined. First, the market is the most devoted servant of science and technology as unlimited means of growth and increasing productivity. And who can argue with the logic of this marriage? The market, a dose of democratic institutions, and science and technology have fueled the most rapid and expansive advance in wealth and living standards for more people than the human race has ever known. The power and appeal of the market are so vast that it is almost impossible, and certainly utopian, to imagine any other successful form of human social organization for modern mass society. Even if we factor out the most glaring appeals to raw human greed, what is left is augmented growth. The market argues that growth is always good because it can provide more things and services to more and more people. However, environmentalists suggest that we have another word to describe unchecked growth: cancer.

Second, this growth mentality is wedded to the belief that any problems of a technical nature, such as the environment, can be solved through the market and its twin genies, science and technology. The belief is that once we are faced with a real problem, the magic and invisible hand of the market moves capital and talent toward solving the problem. We develop all kinds of environmentally safe companies that are dedicated to cleaning up the world and making it a sustainable place for our children. Some of these firms even quote the Iroquois adage that before you act, you need to think ahead seven full generations. If we could really think ahead seven generations, that would be wonderful. But in a world where even the most advanced computer becomes second rate within about six months, the idea of thinking ahead 210 years seems utopian in the extreme. In any event, there is a serene faith in the ability of money to solve any problem when it is linked to appropriate science and technology.

What is never questioned is the mentality of unceasing growth as the basic engine of human progress. This is the fundamental metaphysical axiom of the market. Grow or die. Environmentalists disagree, or at least they ask us to ponder this first principle as a way forward toward human flourishing in the next millennium. While many ecologists are not against growth per se, they are cautious about just how much and what kind of growth the world can now sustain. Is there a limit to the carrying capacity of the globe? One thing seems certain. If we think of growth in the market sector as creating a world where everyone will attain a consumptive lifestyle like that of North America and Europe, we will be in deep trouble. There simply may not be enough renewable and nonrenewable resources for everyone to have a life modeled on the suburbs of Los Angeles, London, Tokyo, or Paris.

One immediate possible solution would be to try to redistribute the wealth of the world more equitably for the benefit of all people. There are even some national models for this. In Canada, the richer provinces transfer funds to the poorer provinces. Like all people, the richer provinces grumble about the transfer, but it does provide an improved quality of life for the poorer regions of the country. However, I see little chance of the Canadian interprovincial transfer of wealth being feasible on the international stage. On the contrary, the present trend is for the rich countries to get richer and the poor poorer. This is precisely why the poorer and less developed countries of the South are not eager to limit any profitable form of industrial development, no matter how detrimental to the environment.

The root cause, as the Buddhists and Confucians keep reminding us, is our desire for more. Until and unless we can curb this desire for more, it is hard to see how we are going to solve the problem of overconsumption and its terrible impact on the environment. As Sagan pointed out, this is a problem of core human values that goes right to the heart of religious ethics. It is not enough merely to appeal to enlightened self-interest, that is to say, to change our patterns of consumption or risk environmental catastrophe. We desperately need a new earth ethic.

This has been a grim picture so far. The earth is suffering; the poor of the earth are suffering; and the only appeal seems to be the hope for a fundamental reorientation of human nature. Or, if you place your faith in the market as a social force, in modernization and economic growth. Fat chance, many will say. Just look at what happened in China when Mao Tse-tung tried to change human nature in order to create a perfect Marxist society. The Chinese are still suffering from the mistakes of Mao's enthusiasm for reforming human nature. It is just this kind of social engineering run amok that frightens people and makes them want to leave the question of consumption to the neutral and hidden hand of the market.

Is there anything hopeful that we can point to? Or is all gloom and doom? Hardly. Many secular and religious organizations are hard at work around the world trying to find solutions to our collective problems. One of the most impressive aspects of these efforts is the cooperation at all levels of religious and ethnic divides. It seems to have dawned on all but the most recalcitrant that there is no possible way for just one group to save the world. Even if the Christian churches made the environment their chief theological and practical issue globally, this would only represent perhaps a third of humankind. The same can be said for all the other religions as well. There is a growing recognition across the religious spectrum that the environment is one issue that needs to be tackled collectively if we are to be successful at all.

One of the most promising yet complicated ventures has been the global interreligious process of advising in the composition of the draft of the international Earth Charter. The preamble of the draft of the charter states:

> In our diverse yet increasingly interdependent world, it is imperative that we, the people of Earth, declare our responsibility to one another, to the greater community of life, and to future generations. We are one human family and one Earth community with a common destiny . . .
>
> Having reflected on these considerations, we recognize the urgent need for a shared vision of basic values that will provide an ethical foundation for the emerging world community. We, therefore, affirm the following principles for sustainable development. We commit ourselves as individuals, organizations, business enterprises, communities, and nations to implement these interrelated principles and to create a global partnership in support of their fulfillment.

If all goes well, the Earth Charter will be submitted to the United Nations General Assembly in the year 2000. The ecological crisis of the past three decades has become an international legal and moral concern. The United Nations began to debate appropriate responses with the Stockholm Conference on the Human Environment in 1972.

Traditionally the United Nations has been concerned, having been formed after the Second World War, with the question of global peace and security. However, the diplomats of the United Nations realized that there can be no peace without securing human rights for all peoples. Slightly later the question of how social and economic development rights and conventions should be linked to the agenda of human rights as a way to achieve international peace and security was added to the United Nations debates. And last, but not least, after 1972 it became apparent that peace and security, human rights, and sustainable development needed to be seen in the context of the environmental crisis. At the same time that the United Nations began to debate about the environment, the churches of the World Council of Churches and the Vatican also conferred their attention upon the environmental crisis.

The draft of the Earth Charter (i.e., the working Draft II of April 1999; the final version will probably differ from the 1999 draft because the charter is still very much a work in progress) was framed against a whole series of consultations with the faith communities of humankind. It is a difficult task to find language that will speak to a Buddhist, Jew, Christian, Muslim, Hindu, Confucian, Taoist, Sikh, Jain, Native elder, and so on. One of the criticisms of the draft charter is that it does not sing or soar to moral heights because it has been written by a committee. Another complaint is that the charter can only reflect the lowest common denominator possible for people concerned about the earth. All of this is true, but it should not obscure the fact that the charter's drafting has been done in extensive consultation with the religious communities.

The Earth Charter is a short document of barely three printed pages. It is symbolically built around sixteen statements of principle for action into the new millennium. It concludes with the following statement of purpose as article 16: "Create a culture of peace and responsibility." The aim of the whole enterprise is to urge the United

Nations to adopt the charter, giving it a legal standing in the world community. Although the charter would not have the force of international and national law, it would begin the process of moving environmental issues from debate to the sphere of law.

If the Earth Charter is adopted by the United Nations and taken seriously by the international community, this will bespeak success for a major interfaith initiative. Take the first principle: "Respect Earth and all life." The second and fourth articles state: "Care for the community of life in all its diversity" and "Secure Earth's abundance and beauty for present and future generations." In the case of Christian thought, these principles demand a new theology of ecological respect as an advance over the old theory of human domination of nature. Of course, biblical scholars now tell us that the Hebrew word translated as "domination" really means something more like responsible stewardship instead of ruthless control. Nonetheless, generations of Christians have listened to the siren voice of the "domination of nature" as a warrant for doing anything they liked to the natural world. This included not even granting any intrinsic dignity to the other living things of the world.

Furthermore, article 7 proposes an ecological golden rule: "Treat all living beings with compassion, and protect them from cruelty and wanton destruction." Here the concerns for sustainable eco-justice are enunciated, and there are other even more specific injunctions. For instance, article 3 states: "Strive to build free, just, participatory, sustainable and peaceful societies." If this is still too vague, articles 10 and 14 proclaim "Eradicate poverty, as an ethical, social, economic, and ecological imperative," and "affirm and promote gender equality as a prerequisite to sustainable development." The drafters of the charter obviously listened with care to the voices of minority and poor people around the world. I also like to think that they listened to the most compassionate and moral of the world's religious leaders as well.

The voices of Jewish, Christian, and Muslim prophets sound their clarion call in these and other principles of environmental social justice. At the middle of article 10 in a subtheme, the charter concretely urges the need to "Generate opportunities for production and meaningful employment." Furthermore, the charter presses on in a subtheme to article 14 to argue that we must "Establish the full and equal participation of women in civil, cultural, economic, political, and social life." Broad as this principle sounds, it will probably clash with the teachings of many conservative religious communities. For instance, as I have already noted before, one of the most reliable ways to deal with the excess growth in population is to provide women with education and economic and social security. Educated and empowered women make sensible choices as an aggregate about population issues. Unfortunately, this clashes with conservative male religious leadership that is only too willing to tell women what they must do with their souls, wills, minds, and bodies.

The Earth Charter strives to address all three of the great ecological questions, namely, consumption, population, and economic development. It challenges the nations and religions of the world to live up to their highest ideals. No religion teaches that people should be forced to live in abject poverty with little control over the economic, political, social, and cultural forces that shape their lives. Of course, there is a special calling for spiritual poverty in many religions. There is also the calling for celibacy, but the twin virtues of voluntary poverty and celibacy are gifts only when they are truly voluntary. There is nothing gracious about a child dying of thirst or disease. This is a mockery of the kind of true spiritual poverty that is a service to others, the love of Christ and the compassion of Buddha—every religion will have its special word for this special humane virtue of loving compassion. As Islam teaches, God is merciful. The charter ends by recording that

> As never before in human history, common destiny beckons us to redefine our priorities and to seek a new beginning. Such renewal is the promise of the Earth Charter principles, which are the outcome of a worldwide dialogue in search of common ground and shared values. Fulfillment of this promise depends upon our expanding and deepening the global dialogue. It

requires an inner change—a change of heart and mind. It requires that we take decisive action to adopt, apply, and develop the vision of the Earth Charter locally, nationally, regionally, and globally. Different cultures and communities will find their own distinctive ways to express the vision, and we will have much to learn from each other. . . .

We can, if we will, take advantage of the creative possibilities before us and inaugurate an era of fresh hope. Let ours be a time that is remembered for an awakening to a new reverence for life, a firm commitment to restoration of Earth's ecological integrity, a quickening of the struggle for justice and empowerment of the people, cooperative engagement of global problems, peaceful management of change, and joyful celebration of life. We will succeed because we must.

One of the great debates between and among religions today focuses on views of the reproductive rights of women. The liberal elements in all the religions have not only accepted the liberation of women but have applauded it as the end of the Neolithic domination of men over women. I mean Neolithic literally. My good friend and mentor Professor Ursula Franklin of the University of Toronto was once talking to me and a group of young women scholars about her and their struggle to be accepted as full participants in the academy. Ursula herself did not begin teaching till well into her distinguished career because in the 1950s and early 1960s it was unheard of for a woman to teach in an engineering school.

Professor Franklin made a general observation about the religions of the world. Most of the young women present were from Christian backgrounds, and they were uniformly unhappy with what they perceived as the hostility of the Christian tradition to their search for full humanity. Ursula made the comment that they should not be too hard on Christianity (she herself is a pillar of the Quaker community) for its sins. As she said, and I paraphrase from a clear memory, "It has been downhill for women in all the religions ever since the Neolithic." Ursula went on to note that it would be counterproductive to blame any one religion for a general trend in all the new civilizations of the world that emerged from the Neolithic world and the later agricultural and urban revolutions.

Professor Franklin noted that there was now a general reversal of the denigration and oppression of women that marked the end of the Neolithic world and the rise of what we call "civilization." The task was now for women to demand reform in the old structures of oppression. One of the areas that must be addressed is family planning. This is important not only for the individual life of each woman but for the survival of the planet. However, this is a difficult new realization for many traditional religions. In the past, for instance, Christianity, Hinduism, Confucianism, and Islam approved of large families. This was not without merit in a world where the only sound form of social insurance was a large and prosperous family. But today to continue a pro-natal policy as if it were the divine will of God is a mistake. In an overpopulated world we must devise new and creative ways to ensure the well-being of the orphan, the elderly, the sick, the widowed, and the poor.

By now some readers may be wondering why I have spent so much time writing about the changing roles of women since Neolithic times. The reason is that many feminist historians of religion have noted that women are often linked metaphorically with nature in religious discourse. For instance, when we talk about the earth in affectionate terms, we say Mother Earth. When we are worried about how our human actions affect the world around us, we say that it is not nice to fool Mother Nature. Because of the connection of the image of earth and nature with the feminine, when either women or the earth are despised or merely ignored, there is a need to revalorize fundamental views of both women and nature. This kind of joint partnership is precisely what is happening these days. It is no longer acceptable to harm either women or nature in the name of some High Male Sky God.

Furthermore, the whole ecological crisis is so vast that it needs the concerted attention of all humanity, including both sexes. Religions will need to play their part along with secular scientists, artists, and politicians in trying to reverse present destructive ecological trends. It does not take very long to see how religiously interconnected the modern environmental movement is. North American poets like Gary Snyder make use of Buddhist imagery and stories, along with a profound respect for the teachings of Native religions, to write wonderful poems like the "Smokey the Bear Sutra." Snyder challenges us to reconsider our views of nature and to find a more organic perspective on the world around us. What is powerful about Snyder's vision is its poetic cadence, its visions of a new world in the New World if we would just take the time to listen to nature and to care about it.

On the other side of the world, the fearless Buddhist social activist Sulak Sivaraksa is leading the fight against the destruction of the remaining forests of Thailand. Sulak notes that once the forests of North America can no longer supply America's need for wood, especially wonderful and rare hardwoods, there will be a massive attack on the remaining South Asian forests (as well as on the Amazon rainforests) to supply the demand. In the summer of 1998, Sulak and others were arrested for blocking the construction of a pipeline and road through the virgin forests of northern Thailand. Sulak has spoken eloquently as an engaged Buddhist social activist about the need for Buddhists to develop a new ecological consciousness based on fundamental Buddhist ethical teachings. When questioned about the Buddhist sources of his work, Sulak is a brilliant expositor of the Thai Theravada tradition. But he is cheerful in also acknowledging his debt to Christian liberation theology and social action in the world. He urges his fellow Buddhists to learn from the international and interreligious legacy of responsible and nonviolent forms of protest. Martin Luther King, Jr., was a student of Gandhi, who was a student of Hindu and Buddhist thought. Now, in his turn, an engaged Buddhist such as Sulak is a student of Gandhi and King and has returned the ecological inspiration of early Buddhism to the forests of Thailand via modern India and America.

The list of environmental protest in Asia could be extended to fill many volumes. For instance, Indian ecological activists are working to stop the cutting of the remaining forests of the subcontinent. Another favorite target of these engaged Hindu ecologists is the various massive projects to dam the rivers of India. Hindu ecological leaders combine current analyses of environmental sciences with the ancient reverence that Indians feel for their rivers. From the Hindu viewpoint, the rivers are literal embodiments of the divine reality. To tamper with them is to tamper with the gods themselves. It should be noted that all the religious communities of India—Hindu, Muslim, Buddhist, Sikh, Christian, Jain, and Tribal—are working together to solve the ecological crisis and seek more just and sustainable forms of economic and social development for future generations. Many ecologists argue that how India and China decide to deal with the environment will determine whether or not humanity is a viable species.

The ecological crisis demands a complete revision of our worldviews. This is a most difficult task, even more difficult than changing religious affiliation. Worldviews form the way we look at the world. They, as we saw in chapter 2, are the lenses we view reality through, and they are so close to us that we cannot even see them. When we think about what is normal, matter-of-fact, something not to be doubted, this is a worldview. When we think about what makes for a good argument, this is our worldview. Changing action depends on changing our worldviews. For instance, if we have a market and consumerist worldview that is predicated on continued growth and the linked notion that science and technology can solve any problem in the environment, then there is little impetus for change. The worldview holds that the free market and science will solve all the ecological problems of the modern world. When we link the skill of the market economy to provide us with more and more of the things we desire, there is also little reason to change our fundamental attitudes toward nature. And last but not least, when all of these worldviews are joined to the religious conviction that we human beings are truly not of this world anyway, it is almost impossible to see what can be done to save the world.

Yet change we must. I believe that the transformation of our ecological worldview is also linked to the reformation of our religious worldviews. When we look at the pictures from the Hubble space telescope, we realize how vast the universe is. We are now even discovering that there are planets circling other suns in our own galaxy, and no doubt, other galaxies. This is not the cozy little triple-decker house of the writers of the early biblical narratives wherein our planet was at the center of creation. We are also now intensely aware of other religions. We are not alone. It is time for us to acknowledge both of these facts and find ways to act on the reality of the vastness of the cosmos and the diversity of human religion in terms of love, wisdom, and action. The earth and our own viability as a species await our decisions.

CHAPTER 7

Coffee at the Remainder of the Day

Regular, Flavored, or Decaf?

What kind of coffee do you drink at the remainder of the day? Just as in the case of religious matters, there are so many choices today. Do you want decaf or regular? Hazelnut or cappuccino? Has the world of religion, once so firm and secure, been transformed into a divine deli, a supermarket of religious values on sale in today's market? Of course, the more cynical theological critic can suggest that all I have done, by painting a positive vision of the new religious pluralism and personal boundary crossing, is make a virtue out of necessity. The truly annoyed conservative theologian reminds me that this easy accommodation with cultural fads and cults happened in Germany and allowed the Nazis to traduce the Christian churches. Only later did deluded Christians rue the day they ever deviated from the straight and narrow path of orthodox righteousness. The criticism, based on history, theology, and sociology, deems that all I have done is describe what had been going on in North American religious life, albeit from a liberal perspective. This is merely pandering to the fads of the time. True religion is not about fads; it is about truth and salvation, liberation and forgiveness, grace and a strangely warmed heart. I disagree that I have merely pandered to the times, although I agree that religion must be about salvation and truth.

Somehow, such a challenge to contemporary religious pluralism appears misdirected. The yoga teacher down the street, the Islamic center over on the west side of town, and the Buddhist meditation hall share no discernible characteristics with the terrors of the atavistic Nazis. The great neo-orthodox preachers of the middle of the twentieth century fought against Hitler. I often wonder what Karl Barth would have made of Gandhi if the two men had ever been in a retreat center for a week of conversation. Barth denounced demonism wherever he saw it. Would Barth have seen a demon in Gandhi? On the contrary, Howard Thurman and Martin Luther King, Jr., both saw in Gandhi someone who could teach them more about their Christian faith.

Closer to home, Muslims remind anyone who is interested that the Arabic term *Islam* means peace in English. The newer religious teachers in North America have come to teach their people and to offer their practices and faith to anyone who wants to listen. People are listening because they hear something of the divine harmony in what they are learning from others. As in so many areas, Martin Luther King, Jr., was ahead of his times in his admiration for other religions; yet no one doubts King's profound commitment to the Christian gospel. As surely as it has happened in the past, religious wanderers will return home with new gifts for those who did not make the journey with them. King did this after his trip to India to honor the memory of Gandhi. Christianity will change; Christianity has always changed, and sometimes for the better, as King's civil rights movement demonstrated.

In academic terms, I stand accused of confusing factual description of what is happening with normative discourse about what religious people ought to believe. The problem with this confusion is that theology has always been considered a normative discourse, not merely another way of describing what is happening around us.

Another way of putting the issue is the thesis that you can't derive "ought" from the mere "is" of the present empirical reality. Of course, my critic pounces on the fact that I have resolutely sought to focus attention on the reality of the present religious situation rather than decrying its imperfections. The conservative argument is that I should better use my skills to preach a reformation of modern life so that it conforms more closely to the historic paradigm of Christian faith rather than the other way around. I contend that we cannot return to Calvin's Geneva, and why would we want to? Do we want to burn theologians anymore because we disagree with them? The Supreme Court would object to the immolation of theologians on the basis of the fundamental right of free speech and the separation of church and state; due process probably would find a place in the Court's opinion as well. Do we want to return to slavery, the oppression of women, the persecution of our Jewish brothers and sisters? Haven't we learned to do better?

I have a dual defense to the charge of merely preaching modernity qua religious pluralism as the gospel. The first is that I do not believe that theology is just the application of the study of Christian history to the present, changing reality. I do not subscribe to what W. C. Smith calls the "Big Bang" theory of the origin and worthiness of religious life. Smith's thesis is that many religious people believe that the closer you can get to the origin or founder of your particular tradition, the more faithful you are. A good example of this is the Protestant veneration of the Bible and historical studies. If you can no longer interview a living Jesus, you look to the book that records his incarnation, ministry, and passion. Protestants argue that they are being faithful to the Christian faith because they are trying to discover what Jesus and the early disciples really did and taught. Protestants reject reliance on church tradition as a means of leading a true Christian life because it is further from the life, death, and resurrection of Jesus. Of course, this quest for the historical Jesus of the Bible merely replaces one tradition, let us say of Orthodox veneration of the early fathers and councils of the church and the Roman Catholic emphasis on tradition in general, with the Protestant veneration of biblical texts. This Protestant argument always seems odd to Orthodox and Roman Catholic Christians because they perceive immediately that their Protestant friends are merely exchanging one tradition, namely, the use of the Bible to discover the will of God, for other traditions.

However, there is one trait that links all these ways of seeking reliable information about the early Jesus movement. It is the belief that, like distance from the sun, you get colder over time as you move away from the life of the founder, in this case, the Son of God. W. C. Smith thinks that this is an odd argument for the Protestant traditions, which pride themselves on their monotheistic theologies. If God is really God, how can God be any more distant from modern people than the disciples of Jesus or even St. Paul, who never actually met the living Jesus? Smith's point is that all Christians are equally close to or distant from God. Or as the Muslims say, God is closer to us than our jugular vein.

From the Christian viewpoint, why bother with the Holy Spirit if we are doomed to know less and less about God the greater the distance in time between us and the incarnation and passion of Jesus, whom we confess as the Christ? In fact, the logic of this kind of "origins are best" argument should make us despair as we individually grow older and hence further by the minute from the life, teachings, and passion of Jesus. Of course, there are some Protestant theologians who say, Precisely; there is nothing that we can do about our own salvation because it depends solely and completely on God's grace. Because of original sin, we are so corrupted as human beings that we cannot rely on any human means for our salvation.

Let us accept, for the moment, the main thrust of this typical Protestant theological argument for the "total depravity" of human nature. It is not even a unique doctrine. The Japanese Pure Land Buddhists also argue that, because of the corrupt nature of the times, we must open ourselves to the amazing grace of Amida's primal vow to save all sentient creatures. Let us accept original sin and our fallen nature in need of God's grace (or that the causal chain of evil karma makes both our social reality and individual natures corrupt). Nonetheless, God (or the Buddha), we are taught, still acts in the world to redeem us. That is why there is all this language about God being a loving father to humanity. How does regeneration, sanctification, and salvation finally happen for such sinners as we surely are? Did it happen once and for all in the incarnation and passion of Jesus? But then, how does it happen in our lives today? We still have to develop a doctrine of God's grace (read action) for modern people in a religiously plural world. W. C. Smith argues that it would simply be easier if we recognize that the doctrine of the Holy Spirit teaches that God is as close to each of us today as God was to the disciples of Jesus in the garden in Jerusalem. In the story of divine love and salvation, time and distance mean nothing to God, who is truly the Lord of Creation.

All of this means that history, though important, is not the final source of good theology. We cannot simply apply the lessons of the past in the hope that they will work for us today. Theology is not history. Theology is the action of the Spirit of God in the lives of people today, confronting their own unique problems. Of course, history is important, too. But history, like theology, changes over time. At present, our historical consciousness is formed by contemporary standards of critical inquiry and science. Biblical studies are one of the last bastions of scientistic positivism long abandoned in other areas of academic research; these studies argue that we can know about matters of faith based on the "objective" and "rational" grounds of scientific modes of historical and social research.

We need traditions to guide us and conform us in our practice and piety as we test our lives and culture, the fruit of the spirit, against the honored records of the saints. Most of us desperately need our religious traditions just like a boat needs a good keel to safely navigate the storms of life. Again on the other side of the world, the Confucian tradition argues that the sages wrote the sacred books because heaven does not speak to us save as the cosmic book of nature. The records of the sages are as close as we can get to a record of the Mandate of Heaven. Be this Christian and Confucian argument as it may, it is still the case that the recorded history of Christianity will not help us sail into new harbors when we encounter them on our journeys of faith. The Confucian scholars, who were extremely historically oriented, argued that only the sage can navigate on her or his own; the rest of us desperately need to check our intuitions against the teachings of true worthies and sages. If we read the histories of the sages we will at least know that people encounter new things in history even if we do not know just what to do in our particular confrontations with the newness of change. Jesus reminded his disciples that none save God is holy, and Confucius taught his disciples that he was not a sage; both the Christ and the Teacher of the Ten Thousand Generations (one of the best titles for Confucius) tried to inculcate some intellectual humility into their unruly flocks.

The experience of the present is a vital source for theology when it is creatively joined to the record of the past. We must learn from the present; we must savor its lessons. However, this does not simply mean that we accept everything in the present. For instance, basic human decency, the love of God and neighbor more than the love of self, are pretty good summaries of these teachings. These teachings forbid us to accept anything less worthy as innovations for conduct and piety. The experience of the German people with the Nazi movement and the Chinese experience with the terrors of the Cultural Revolution provide perfect examples of what should be rejected merely because it is new and exciting. Evil can be exciting, sometimes more thrilling than mundane good. Some Red Guards have told me that it was more fun to roam around China cursing their teachers and elders than to attend school in the '60s and '70s. However, older and now wiser, former Red Guards see themselves as a lost generation, a generation without the educational skills needed for their own lives and for the development of modern China. As they now say, the Cultural Revolution was neither a revolution nor cultural. The keel of history must remind us that worthy religious movements, and the changes they seek, are always moral in intent. The lure of evil is to be resisted.

The second response to the use of the present religiously plural situation in the debate between the descriptive and normative nature of theology depends on my thesis that descriptive and normative judgments actually belong together in some cases. Resistance to the Nazis is again a good example. Having witnessed the actions of the

Nazis, a grand coalition arose to defeat Hitler and his armies. It was precisely those liberal, pluralistic societies of the United Kingdom, Canada, Australia, and the United States (with a great deal of help from the Soviet Union, the totalitarian exception) that destroyed the Nazi menace and its imperial Japanese allies. I find it fascinating that we remember in American seminaries the German theologians who struggled against Hitler but fail to honor my father and his generation of conservative and liberal Christians, atheists, Jews, Buddhists, and many, many more, who actually defeated the fascists. We should honor the memory of the German martyrs but also never forget that it was the democratic, liberal, pluralistic countries, along with the Soviets, who defeated Hitler. Without the despised tolerant liberals around the world, the few German theologians would all have been exterminated in concentration camps. With all due respect to everyone who denounced the Nazis, Barth and Tillich never went to war against Hitler; my father's generation in the Atlantic and Pacific did the heavy lifting against the Germans and Japanese.

Sometimes there is nothing so fierce, paraphrasing Oliver Cromwell's comment about Presbyterians during the English Civil War, as a liberal pluralist freshly risen from prayer. The Germans and Japanese painted a disparaging picture of the "mongrel" American forces and society. Of course, the Allies were flawed as well because of their bigotry against people of color at home and in their empires. But the Japanese and Germans learned that these "mongrels" could fight for human dignity with utter success in the end. The people of England, Australia, France, occupied Europe, and North America had no trouble fusing description and normative theory and action; tolerance, liberalism, and openness to others do not mean a lack of courage or conviction.

Considering the moral convictions and open worldview of liberal religious pluralism, I now believe that the description of the emerging diverse religious worlds of North America tells us something normative about theology. The simple fact is that God creates and sustains a plural world wherein different religions wax and wane over time and space. Others will point out that we have always lived in a pluralistic world. The Jesus movement was born in such a milieu in the eastern Mediterranean. To fast-forward to the present, there has been a great deal of Christian history since the first Jewish disciples, St. Paul as the founder of the mission to the gentiles, and the early conversion of the Greeks, Romans, and Germanic peoples.

For our purposes, it is best to pick up the story at the end of the eighteenth and the beginning of the nineteenth century with the Protestant mission to the world, or the wilderness of paganism as they saw it. In fact, it is in the area of mission that the whole question of religious pluralism is the most vexing. One of the cherished goals of the modern Christian movement was to preach the gospel to the four corners of the globe. It was highly successful in doing this. To remind ourselves again of this history, at the beginning of the 1790s with William Carey's mission to India, Christians probably comprised about 6 percent of the world's population. Although accurate religious statistics are hard to come by, the best estimate now is that Christians are around 32 percent of the people of the world. Along with this numerical growth, Christians are now found on every continent. What was basically a European religion at the beginning of the nineteenth century, along with outposts in the Americas, has become a truly global religion.

But every success has a dark side. Along with decent European missionaries came plagues plus empire builders who had nothing but contempt for the Native peoples of the Americas, Africa, and the Pacific Rim. Empire was also part of what modern ecologists call the "Neo-European" travel kit. For instance, the Americas were jointly conquered by the new nation-states of Europe, their improved military skills, and their diseases. Ecologically and agriculturally, the European immigrants brought with them their dogs, cattle, pigs, sheep, plants, diseases, and trees. Furthermore, in the eighteenth and nineteenth centuries, these Europeans, as they swarmed over the Americas, also developed sophisticated industrial civilizations. But what has been the potential ecological price to be paid by the success of the Neo-European peoples?

What price do modern Neo-European Christians pay when they

have gained the world and created the conditions for an ecological catastrophe? Christians are proud of the fact that they are now the largest religion in the world. But are we equally proud of the fact that Christendom as a culture might well have destroyed the capacity for the planet to sustain humanity into the next millennium? Is Christianity a viable religion without repentance for the consequences of its historical success in the last five centuries? Christians are proud of the growth of the church but may yet rue the day of unchecked growth because of the ecocrisis that is this growth's unanticipated stepchild.

The intent of the early missionaries was not only to preach the gospel to everyone but to convert the world to Christianity. For instance, one of the main goals of the movement in the late nineteenth century was to make the twentieth into "the Christian century." In many ways the twentieth century was a Christian century, but not quite as had been anticipated. As Max Weber noted long before, the success of any social movement has unanticipated consequences. We have already chronicled in chapter 6 the present concern for the unbalanced ecology caused by the expansion of Neo-European empire, commerce, and industrialization neatly now called development and globalization. However, in Asia, the home of other great religions, the Christian mission sparked indigenous renewals of Islam, Buddhism, Hinduism, Sikhism, Jainism, Shintoism, Taoism, and Confucianism. The revival of the Asian traditions led, especially for Hinduism and Buddhism, to new missions of their own to Europe and North America. One of the outcomes of all these missionaries coming and going is that Buddhism and Islam are the most rapidly growing religions in North America.

Accompanying the renewal of ancient Asian religions in Asia itself, there now comes the massive movement of Asian people into North America after the repeal of earlier racist immigration laws after 1965. Although not as massive as the migration of the Neo-European peoples in the nineteenth and early twentieth centuries, the movement of Asian peoples into North America may well mean that the twenty-first will be the Pacific Rim century. Most definitely the face of North American religion will never be the same.

But as I have emphasized before, the world has always been religiously pluralistic. In this regard, I remember hearing a Chinese Christian leader talk about his experiences of reopening the Chinese churches after the demise of the Maoist Cultural Revolution and the major Chinese social and economic reforms in 1979. When he was asked if there was anything good to say about the Cultural Revolution, he remarked that there was nothing good to say about it because of the pain it caused the Chinese people individually and as a society. But he did reflect that when he was banished to the country during the Cultural Revolution because of his Christian faith, he did have a lot of time to think about his theology and discuss it with the various communist officials who were also attacked and exiled during the 1960s and 1970s. One of the things that came to mind, he said, was the biblical statement about the church becoming the salt of the world. He decided that this definitely did not mean that the whole world should become one huge salt lick. The world did not need this kind of religious uniformity. It needed the Christian churches, yes, but not as some new hegemonic reality designed to crush the spirits of everyone else.

One of the things my Chinese friend reaffirmed was that the world is pluralistic and obviously will remain so. It is time for Christians to grow up and recognize this reality. It will not go away. In fact, the more that Christians push, the more this will strengthen the resolve of members of the other religions to do better in their own missions. Now, this is not entirely an unhappy outcome if this new mission of the religions of the world is done in charity, love, respect, and compassion. For instance, we have already argued that the ecological issues are a perfect arena for interreligious cooperation. Work with international refugees, confronting racism and xenophobia, economic development, and international peace and security issues are more areas in which religions can play a positive role if they want.

However, this kind of cooperation will remain facile and half-hearted until and unless it is done with real respect. If the final aim of this proximate cooperation is merely to set the other person up for conversion to your own tradition, it will hardly work at the end of the day. People are not that stupid. It does not take them long to ferret out the real motives of any mission. Those missionaries that come with love and charity, plus real respect, become the friends of the people and, dare I say, the friends of God. The Muslims have a wonderful saying about this matter. The prophet Muhammad was once asked about the role of competition between Muslims and Christians. The Prophet replied that there is only one kind of merited competition between religious people, and that is the struggle to do good works. Let Muslims and Christians compete in creating a better world together; according to the great Prophet of Islam, this is the only worthy competition between people of faith. Some good, sharp theological debate adds spice to the undertaking, but only as long as good works remain fixed in the minds of the missionaries. But what about mission as proclamation and invitation?

I have also learned to appreciate another Islamic insight. There should be no compulsion in religion. This ought to become the guiding principle of all interreligious work, including missions, in the next millennium. In a recent Muslim-Christian dialogue, a version of this teaching was extended to mission theory. I think that it is one of the best definitions of mission I have ever heard, although it is very brief: True dialogue, true mission should protect *the right to convince and be convinced*. The rest is God's work. Each person should have the utter freedom to make their own informed decision about what they have heard in religious debate. Mission is no longer a monologue of the missionary with a target audience that is never invited to share their insights with the missionary. There is an element of freedom to be preserved in the dialogical conversation. It may be the case that the other person makes a better presentation. The right to convince and be convinced lies at the heart of religious mission, proclamation, and dialogue.

The Confucian philosopher Tu Wei-ming has argued recently that Confucius's negative version of the Golden Rule, namely, do not do to others what you do not want done to you, is a highly effective way to frame this crucial ethical insight in a pluralistic society. Tu presses the point that the positive version of the Golden Rule, when it is linked to a crusading mentality that knows it is right and that everyone else is wrong, can become highly authoritarian. It is an easy step from trying to do good for others to believing that the others are not good and worthy people if they do not see your good as their good. The negative version of the Golden Rule has a different inner logic. You do not want people to force their customs on you, so you should extend the same courtesy to everyone else even if you think that they are mistaken from time to time.

Actually, something just like this happened during the great Western missionary movement of the preceding two centuries. Many missionaries went out to Asia knowing nothing of Asian culture or religion. They thought that the proper Christian teaching was to despise the religions of the Asian people. However, as they learned more and more about the religions of Asia, these great missionary scholars began to change their minds. They were the first Western intellectuals to actually learn something about Asian religions firsthand. They invented the study of the history of religion. As they studied Buddhism, Sikhism, Jainism, Confucianism, and Taoism, they grew to respect these religious traditions. It is fascinating to read their reports to the famous missionary congress held in Edinburgh in 1910. Written in the elegant, wonderful prose of Edwardian England, the reports from the field shine with a respect for the peoples of the world.

Of course, these pioneers of intercultural exchange in 1910 did not give up their calling to proclaim the gospel in Asia. It is hard to see how anyone from their time and background could have done so; moreover, there is a persistent, nay even normative, demand in the Christian tradition to share the story of Jesus. The real debate is not over proclamation but rather about how this is to be done. But the early missionaries certainly had learned to do so with respect and even high admiration for what they found in the religious life of the people of Asia. More and more these missionaries realized that honest, sincere, and respectful dialogue was the only real way forward in interreligious encounters. The best of these missionaries understood that they could not and should not presume to confuse the secular power of the modern Western world with the message of the gospel. The gospel was not a better gunboat full of Western military power.

The first learning, slow to come, was that God had not been absent from Asia, Africa, the Americas, and the vast oceans of the world. The second learning, namely, a positive theology of religious pluralism, has not yet happened for most Christians, though the increasing religious border crossings I have been discussing are having a major impact on how Christians see people of other faiths. It is time for the Christian world to mature enough to be in touch with the noblest parts of its own tradition and recognize that Christians are not alone in God's economy of salvation. It is time that we become self-consciously pluralistic in our theologies. It is fascinating to note that Christian social practice is more and more pluralistic in North America; theology, often the handmaiden of actuality, needs to begin the journey as well. This, of course, is typical of the pragmatic turn of North American intellectual life. North Americans tend to develop a practice first and then figure out the theory that goes with it.

Such a clear-eyed empirical and normative theology is needed by our churches, or at least those Christians who find the distance between the received monological, exclusive teachings and their own positive experience of pluralistic practice becoming a chasm. Christians need to grow up and understand that they are only one part of God's family. I would be the last person to say that this will be an easy task. It flies in the face of a great deal of Christian teaching over the past two thousand years. But just as Christians now abhor slavery and the oppression of women, so too Christians will need to understand their faith in positive relation to other traditions.

Of course, there have been Christian theologies of other religions before. But, for the most part, they have been negative or only proximately positive. Finally, it was assumed that other religions were, however noble, only prologues to the eventual victory of Christianity. At the remainder of the day, all knees would bow to the one true Lord of history.

The problem with maintaining such a theological vision today is that it makes no sense. As we learn more and more about people of other faiths it does little good to pretend that God's spirit has not enlivened their lives. Of course, many Christians will hold to the older position of excluding persons from final salvation and God's eternal love. Only professing Christians, it is maintained, will ultimately be saved from the fire to come. Paradigm shifts that suggest entire new worldviews, such as the positive nature of religious pluralism, are always hard to accept. They are perhaps some of the most difficult things a religious person can do. It demands that we do something new. But then, is that not what religion is about, the new? We can say all we like that religion and faith are about tradition, and that is true. But in the still, quiet moment when we are transformed by the vision of the divine reality, we are made new. It is time that we made new our vision of the world, too.

My suspicion is that this will happen almost without notice. As more and more people cross back and forth from practice to practice as I have recounted here, they will become pluralists even if they are not theologians. They do not even need to give it a name. It will come about simply from the fact that they have learned to live with and appreciate people of other faiths. But the critic might still ask, Can this actually happen? I answer that it already has. For instance, for a majority of Christians in North America, the consensus is that the Jewish community does not need to be converted to the Christian faith in order to share in the Kingdom to come. Of course, this is precisely what the Jewish community has maintained all along, and they must be pleased to see their daughter religion finally awaken to this fact.

Does this mean that Christians have to give up their faith? Not at all. There is no reason for the Christian mission of proclamation to cease. In fact, I wish that more liberal Christians of deep faith and conviction were more willing to share their faith with others. It is a shame that mission and proclamation have become the property of fundamentalists who seek to exclude and make the "good news" the bad news of rejection to anyone beyond the pale of their confessional understanding of God's transforming grace. Christians always have a wonderful, saving story to tell. Christians have Jesus as the Christ and the record of his incarnation, teachings, and passion to share with a weary world. All Christians now need to remember that this mission is God's mission. We cannot tell what impact the story of Jesus will have on people. Some will become Christians. But others will become better Buddhists and Hindus for hearing the story. Who can deny that Mahatma Gandhi was inspired by Jesus? And who can deny that Gandhi did not teach Charlie Andrews, Howard Thurman, and Martin Luther King, Jr., something about the beloved community of all God's children?

What must change is that Christians can take joy, real joy in meeting with people of other faith in order to share their stories. The pluralist conviction is that all the good stories come from God. We can share the good and seek to combat evil. The very notion that there will be only one religion runs against the whole history of God's interaction with the world and its creatures. It is time to share and celebrate. It is time to tell our stories. Each of us has a story and is called and claimed by it. We cannot pretend to know all the stories of God's other creatures. But we can take satisfaction in telling our story well. We can also be faithful to the commandment not to bear false witness against our neighbors. We can then truly seek the way and the truth that surpasses all understanding.

Bibliography

This bibliography is neither exhaustive nor even widely representative of the material concerning the theology of religious pluralism. Rather, I have included, along with works cited, a range of other texts that illustrate my argument for a positive theology of religious pluralism and border crossing between and among the faiths. Further, I have listed some works that are highly critical of this liberal interpretation. I have also added a number of more popular and readable works that can serve as references for further study. To further explain my selections in this very short bibliography, I have annotated some of the titles; further I have marked basic reference works with an asterisk (*).

*Albanese, Catherine L. 1991. *America: Religion and Religions*. 2nd Edition. Belmont, CA: Wadsworth. [The standard modern history of religion in North America; a well-crafted college textbook]

*Ariarajah, Wesley. 1985. *The Bible and People of Other Faiths*. Geneva: The World Council of Churches; Maryknoll, NY: Orbis Books, 1989. [Short work dedicated to reading the Bible faithfully in a pluralistic world; written for a broad audience]

Berger, Peter L. 1998. "Protestantism and the Quest for Certainty." *The Christian Century*. Vol. 115, No. 23 (August 23–September 2, 1998).

*Berling, Judith A. 1997. *A Pilgrim in Chinese Culture: Negotiating Religious Diversity*. Maryknoll, NY: Orbis Books. [Insightful study of Chinese religion and culture for scholars and non-scholars alike]

Berthrong, John H. 1994. *All under Heaven: Transforming Paradigms in Confucian-Christian Dialogue*. Albany, NY: State University of New York Press.

Birch, Charles, and John B. Cobb, Jr. 1981. *The Liberation of Life*. Cambridge: Cambridge University Press. [A foundational theological reflection for ecological concerns]

*Bosch, David J. 1991. *Transforming Mission: Paradigm Shifts in Theology of Mission*. Maryknoll, NY: Orbis Books. [The best work in English on the history and theology of Christian missions]

Braaten, Carl E. 1992. *No Other Gospel! Christianity among the World's Religions*. Minneapolis: Fortress Press. [Strong critique of pluralism and dialogue as modes of proper Christian mission]

Carman, John B. 1994. *Majesty and Meekness: A Comparative Study of Contrast and Harmony in the Concept of God*. Grand Rapids, MI: William B. Eerdmans Publishing Company.

Carson, D. A. 1996. *The Gagging of God: Christianity Confronts Pluralism*. Grand Rapids, MI: Zondervan Publishing House. [A massive conservative rejection of any positive theology of religious pluralism]

Ching, Julia. 1998. *The Butterfly Healing: A Life between East and West*. Maryknoll, NY: Orbis Books.

Clarke, J. J. 1997. *Oriental Enlightenment: The Encounter between Asian and Western Thought*. London and New York: Routledge.

Clooney, Francis X., S. J. 1998. *Hindu Wisdom for All God's Children*. Maryknoll, NY: Orbis Books.

Cobb, John B., Jr. 1982. *Beyond Dialogue: Toward a Mutual Transformation of Christianity and Buddhism*. Philadelphia, PA: Fortress Press. [Classic text about the benefits of dialogue as transformation]

*Collins, Randall. 1998. *The Sociology of Philosophies: A Global Theory of Intellectual Change*. Cambridge, MA: The Belknap Press of Harvard University Press. [Large and controversial history of world thought; pays careful attention to Asian and Western developments]

Cooey, Paula M., William R. Eakin, and Jay B. McDaniel, eds. 1991. *After Patriarchy: Feminist Transformations of World Religions*. Maryknoll, NY: Orbis Books.

*Coward, Harold G. 1987. *Pluralism: Challenge to the World Religions*. Maryknoll, NY: Orbis Books.

Cox, Harvey. 1987. *Turning East*. New York: Simon & Schuster.

Cracknell, Kenneth. *Justice, Courtesy, and Love: Theologians and Missionaries Encountering World Religions*. London: Epworth Press. [Wonderful study of Christian mission to 1910; shows how the missionaries became the first Western historians of religions and how many missionaries learned to appreciate the religions of the world]

Dallmayr, Fred. 1998. *Alternative Visions: Paths in the Global Village*. Lanham, MD: Rowan & Littlefield Publishers, Inc.

D'Costa, Gavin. *Theology and Religious Pluralism: The Challenge of the Other Religions*. Maryknoll, NY: Orbis Books.

*De Barry, Wm. Theodore. 1988. *East Asian Civilizations: A Dialogue in Five Stages.* Cambridge, MA: Harvard University Press. [Modest yet comprehensive study of East Asian culture that takes dialogue as a key for cross-cultural interaction]

Driver, Tom F. 1981. *Christ in a Changing World: Toward an Ethical Christology.* New York: Crossroad.

Eck, Diana L. 1993. *Encountering God: A Spiritual Journey from Bozeman to Banaras.* Boston: Beacon Press.

*———. 1997. *On Common Ground: World Religions in America.* New York: Columbia University Press. [A CD-ROM packed with information about the living reality of religions in America. The standard for years to come; with illustrations, maps, local information, and audio descriptions of practice around the country]

*Fernández-Armesto, Felipe. 1995. *Millennium: A History of the Last Thousand Years.* New York: Scribner. [Excellent ecumenical history of the last thousand years that tries to move beyond just writing about the impact of the West on the rest]

Gernet, Jacques. 1985. *China and the Christian Impact.* Trans. by Janet Lloyd. Cambridge and New York: Cambridge University Press.

Griffiths, Paul J. 1990. *Christianity through Non-Christian Eyes.* Maryknoll, NY: Orbis Books.

*Gross, Rita. 1996. *Feminism and Religion: An Introduction.* Boston: Beacon Press. [Overview of the relationship of modern feminism and religion]

Hanegraaff, Wouter J. 1998. *New Age Religion and Western Culture: Esotericism in the Mirror of Secular Thought.* Albany, NY: State University of New York Press.

Heim, S. Mark, ed. 1998. *Grounds for Understanding: Ecumenical Resources for Responses to Religious Pluralism.* Grand Rapids, MI: William B. Eerdmans Publishing Company.

Hick, John. 1993. *Disputed Questions in Theology and the Philosophy of Religion.* New Haven: Yale University Press.

———. 1995. *A Christian Theology of Religions.* Louisville: Westminster John Knox Press. [A classic text by the most famous pluralist theologian; difficult but rewarding text]

*Hodgson, Peter C. 1994. *Winds of the Spirit: A Constructive Christian Theology.* Louisville: Westminister John Knox Press. [A modern systematic theology that pays attention to the fact that Christians live in a pluralistic world]

Hood, Robert M. 1990. *Must God Remain Greek? Afro Cultures and God Talk.* Minneapolis: Fortress Press.

Huntington, Samuel P. 1996. *The Clash of Civilizations and the Remaking of the World Order.* New York: Simon & Schuster.

*Ingram, Paul O. 1997. *Wrestling with the Ox: A Theology of Religious Experience.* New York: The Continuum Publishing Company. [Another fine introductory text to theology in a world of many faiths]

Jensen, Lionel M. 1997. *Manufacturing Confucianism: Chinese Traditions and Universal Civilization.* Durham, NC: Duke University Press.

Kaufman, Gordon D. 1996. *God-Mystery-Diversity: Christian Theology in a Pluralistic World.* Minneapolis: Fortress Press.

Knitter, Paul F. 1995. *One Earth Many Religions: Multifaith Dialogue and Global Responsibility.* Maryknoll, NY: Orbis Books. [This and the book below are the most recent statement of one of the most important pluralist Christian theologians]

————. 1996. *Jesus and Other Names: Christian Mission and Global Responsibility.* Maryknoll, NY: Orbis Books.

Lakoff, George, and Mark Johnson. 1980. *Metaphors We Live By.* Chicago, IL: The University of Chicago Press.

Lindbeck, George A. 1984. *The Nature of Doctrine: Religion and Theology in a Post Liberal Age.* Philadelphia: The Westminster Press.

Lochhead, David. 1988. *The Dialogical Imperative: A Christian Reflection on Interfaith Encounter.* Maryknoll, NY: Orbis Books.

Maguire, Daniel C., and Larry L. Rasmussen. 1998. *Ethics for a Small Planet: New Horizons on Population, Consumption, and Ecology.* Albany, NY: State University of New York Press. [Short text that does not hold back its punches on the real nature of the ecocrisis and the revolution in religious thought it will take to change things for the better]

*Martinson, Paul Varo. 1987. *A Theology of World Religions: Interpreting God, Self and World in Semitic, Indian, and Chinese Thought.* Minneapolis: Augsburg Publishing House. [Focuses on China as important model of religious pluralism in the modern classical and modern worlds]

*Nakamura, Hajime. 1975. *Parallel Developments: A Comparative History of Ideas.* Tokyo: Kodansha Ltd. [A history of world thought by one of Japan's most famous Buddhist historians]

Nash, James A. 1991. *Loving Nature: Ecological Integrity and Christian Responsibility.* Nashville: Abingdon Press. [Excellent introduction to the ecological crisis for Christians]